Patrick

Joseph Duffy

Patrick

in his own words

Veritas Publications Dublin

First published 1972 by
Veritas Publications
7-8 Lower Abbey Street
Dublin 1

Reprinted 1975

This edition published 1985
Reprinted 1988
Copyright © ✠ Joseph Duffy 1972, 1975, 1985

ISBN 0 86217 174 1

The Latin text of the *Confessio* is Dr Bieler's edition, published in
Classica et Mediaevalia and in *Libri Epistolarum Sancti Patricii Episcopi*
(Dublin 1952), and used by permission of the Irish Manuscripts
Commission. English text and translation of the *Confession* and the
Letter to the Soldiers of Coroticus by Joseph Duffy. *Letter to the Soldiers of
Coroticus* used by kind permission of Irish Messenger Publications.

Biblical quotations are from the *Jerusalem Bible,* as far as Patrick's Latin
allows and are used by permission of Darton, Longman and Todd,
London.

Imprimatur
✠ Kevin McNamara
Archbishop of Dublin
1 April 1985

Nihil Obstat
Richard Sherry D.D.
Censor Deputatus

The *nihil obstat* and *imprimatur* are a declaration that a text is considered
to be free of doctrinal or moral error. They do not necessarily imply
agreement with opinions expressed by the author.

Cover design by Eddie McManus

Printed in the Republic of Ireland by Leinster Leader Ltd.,
Naas, Co. Kildare.

Contents

PART ONE: ST PATRICK'S CONFESSION

INTRODUCTION

Patrick intended his *Confession* for both his
friends and his critics. He wanted them to know
the truth about him when he had left them and
was no longer able to defend himself against the
charges of presumption and incompetence which
were levelled against him. His strong feelings on
the subject, his personal sensitivity and his very
unusual experiences come across clearly in his
writing and convey to us in a moving way the
dynamism and spiritual depth of the man himself.
For all his lack of a flowing Latin style and his
decision to tell his story as far as possible in
biblical idiom, even to the point of obscuring the
meaning at times, Patrick writes with discipline
to a single plan. He traces for us his spiritual
development, in other words he explores method-
ically his understanding of himself as a growing
person coming gradually to maturity of vision and
practical wisdom.

Patrick begins by establishing credibility with
his readers. He takes himself and his work very

seriously and feels it to be his duty to state his
case exactly as he saw it, without regard for
personal prestige or literary pretensions. Chapter
Two narrates his achievement of freedom as a
young man, how he escaped first from the usual
frivolities of boyhood and then from physical
slavery. Patrick could only accept his slavery
because it purified and matured him spiritually
in a way which surprised even himself; otherwise
the very thought of it terrified him and left a
deep scar which never quite disappeared. The third
chapter explains the growth of the great ideal of
his life, his missionary vocation. It is worth noting
that he considered this entirely in the context of
his prayer life and as a lifelong aspiration which
continued after his arrival on Irish soil as a bishop.
Although he is reluctant to write at length on his
missionary labours the final chapter inevitably is
the longest. Patrick realises that in the long run it
is a man's record of service and of wholehearted
dedication to his ideal which proves his worth.

So much for content. The key to the style of
Patrick's story is his own Latin Bible. The whole
texture of his language, apart altogether from the
numerous quotations; his doctrinal emphasis on
the providence of God the Father, on his own
obligation to preach the Good News and on the
guidance of the Spirit; the form and content of
his prayers; all derive unmistakably from a lifetime of biblical meditation. Even more funda-
mental is the working out of the central notion
of Scripture as Divine Revelation, as God's
invitation and man's response.

The hard core of the *Confession* is the series of psychic dreams which Patrick firmly believed brought him divine guidance. His response was, perhaps, less dramatic but more in line with the complications of normal human experience. It was many years before Patrick actually returned to Ireland and even after he came his sponsors had genuine qualms about his suitability for the work. Patrick himself had no illusions about the sheer difficulty of his mission and about the intelligence, effort and courage which were demanded of him to the end.

The distinctive features of Patrick's personality and his appreciation of the Bible are evident from even a casual reading of the *Confession*. How the work should be understood historically is an entirely different question and one which has been vigorously and even heatedly debated in recent years with all the expertise of modern scholarship. Specialists in early Irish history, in late or Vulgar Latin, and in the study of saints' lives, have in turn examined minutely the conventional story which most Irish people learned at school and which derives mainly from the *Life of St Patrick* written by Professor J.B. Bury in 1905. According to this story St Patrick was born in Britain, lived from 389 to 461, began his mission in 432 after a lengthy formation at various centres in Gaul, and personally evangelised the five fifths of Ireland.

Scholars are now inclined to regard these dates as too early for the general context of Irish history and to rule out the lengthy formation in an

academic or even monastic environment. On the
other hand we are assured that there are colloquial
elements in Patrick's Latin which belong to Gaul
before the middle of the fifth century, and the
tradition linking the saint with Auxerre in central
Gaul still commands widespread respect. Indeed
this tradition is as venerable and as well established
as Patrick's See at Armagh itself and there can be
little doubt that the axis between Bishop Germanus
of Auxerre (418-48) and the British Church still
provides the only plausible background from
contemporary history which can be read into the
Confession.

The translation of the *Confession* given here is
a free version which has taken account of the
latest available research of professional scholars.
The acknowledged leading authority in Patrician
studies today is Professor Ludwig Bieler of Univer-
sity College, Dublin, and anyone who wishes to
investigate the problems of interpretation in
more detail should begin with his *Libri Epistolarum
Sancti Patricii Episcopi,* Parts 1 and 2 (Dublin
1952), and *St Patrick and the Coming of
Christianity* (Dublin 1967). I am especially grate-
ful to Bishop Richard Hanson for a copy of his
new literal translation published in *Nottingham
Mediaeval Studies* Vol. XV, 1971, which I have
used with profit.

The Latin text is Dr Bieler's, from the critical
edition published in part I of his *Libri Epistolarum.*
The few minor departures from this text have
been carefully noted. Scriptural quotations are
given in italics and Bieler's emendations shown

by square brackets. The numbers in the text which are also used for footnotes to the English version follow Bieler. In the English version chapter divisions, sub-headings and the sources of direct scriptural quotations are introduced. The quotations follow the Jerusalem Bible as closely as Patrick's Latin allows.

THE CONFESSION

Citizen of the Roman Empire 400 A.D.

[1]I am Patrick, a sinner, the most unlearned of men, the lowliest of all the faithful, utterly worthless in the eyes of many. My father was Calpornius who was a deacon and a son of the priest Potitus. He ministered in a suburb of Bannaven Taberniae where he had a country residence nearby.

CHAPTER 1

GOD'S GIFT MUST BE TOLD

Conversion in captivity

It was there I was taken captive. I was about sixteen years of age at the time and I did not know the true God. I was taken into captivity to Ireland with many thousands of people. We deserved this fate because we had turned away from God; we neither kept his commandments nor obeyed our pastors who used to warn us about our salvation. The Lord's fury boiled over on us and he scattered us among many nations, even to the ends of the earth. This is where I now am, in all my insignificance, among strangers. [2] The Lord there made me aware of my unbelief that I might at last advert to my sins and turn wholeheartedly to the Lord my God. He showed concern for my weakness, and pity for my youth and ignorance; he watched over me before I got to know him and before I was able to distinguish good from evil. In fact he protected me and comforted me as a father would his son. [3] I cannot

be silent then, nor indeed should I, about the
great benefits and grace which the Lord saw fit
to confer on me in the land of my captivity. This
is the way we thank God for correcting us and
taking notice of us: we honour and praise his
wonders before every nation under heaven.

Profession of faith in the Trinity

⁴There is no other God,
there never was and there never will be,
than God the Father
unbegotten and without beginning,
from whom is all beginning,
the Lord of the universe as we have been taught;
and his son Jesus Christ
whom we declare
to have been always with the Father
and to have been begotten spiritually by the Father
in a way which baffles description,
before the beginning of the world,
before all beginning;
and by him are made all things visible and invisible.
He was made man,
defeated death
and was received into heaven by the Father,
who has given him all power over all names
in heaven, on earth, and under the earth;
and every tongue will acknowledge to him
that Jesus Christ is the Lord God.
We believe in him
and we look for his coming soon
as judge of the living and of the dead,

who will treat every man according to his deeds.
He has poured out the Holy Spirit on us
    in abundance,
the gift and guarantee of eternal life,
who makes those who believe and obey
sons of God and joint heirs with Christ.
We acknowledge and adore him
as one God in the Trinity of the holy name.

Reasons for writing

[5]He himself has said through the prophet:
*You can invoke me in your troubles and I will
rescue you, and you shall honour me* (Ps. 50 :
15). He also says: *It is right to reveal and publish
the works of God* (Tob. 12 : 7). [6]Although I am
imperfect in many ways I want my brethren and
relatives to know what kind of man I am, so that
they may understand the aspiration of my life.
[7]I know well the statement of the Lord which he
makes in the psalm: *You will destroy those who
tell lies* (Ps. 5 : 6). He says again: *A lying mouth
deals death to the soul* (Wisd. 1: 11). The same
Lord says in the Gospel: *For every foolish word
men speak, they will answer on the day of
Judgement* (Matt. 12 : 36). [8]I ought therefore to
dread with fear and trembling the sentence of that
day when no one will be able to escape or hide,
but when all of us will have to give an account of
even our smallest sins before the court of the
Lord Christ.

⁹For this reason I long had a mind to write, but held back until now. I was afraid of drawing general gossip on myself because I had not studied like the others who got a thorough grounding in law and theology. They never had to change their medium of speech since childhood but were able rather to improve their mastery of it without interruption, while I, on the other hand, had to express myself in a foreign language. Anyone can see from the style of my writing how little training in the use of words I got. As the wise man says: *By language will be recognised understanding, knowledge and true teaching* (Ecclus. 4 : 24).

¹⁰But what good is an excuse, no matter how genuine, especially since I now presume to take up in my old age what I failed to do as a young man? It was my sins then which prevented me from making my own of what I had read. But who believes me although I should repeat what I said at the beginning?

I was taken captive as a youth, a mere child indeed in the matter of learning, before I knew what to pursue and what to avoid. This is why I blush with shame at this stage and positively quail at exposing my incompetence. I am unable to open my heart and mind to those who are used to concise writing in a way that my words might express what I feel. ¹¹If, indeed, I had been equipped as others were, I would not be silent in making my reparation. And if I now appear presumptuous, considering my ignorance and my slow speech, it is after all written: *The stammering tongues will quickly learn the language of peace* (Is. 32 : 4).

How much more, then, must we earnestly strive, we who are, in the words of Scripture, *a saving letter of Christ to the ends of the earth?* (2 Cor. 3 : 2). The letter may not be elegant but it is most assuredly written in your hearts, not with ink but with the spirit of the living God. The Spirit elsewhere is a witness that even uncultivated ways have been created by the Most High. [12]I am, then, first and foremost unlearned, an unlettered exile who cannot plan for the future. But this much I know for sure. Before I had to suffer I was like a stone lying in the deep mud. Then he who is mighty came and in his mercy he not only pulled me out but lifted me up and placed me at the very top of the wall. I must, therefore, speak publicly in order to thank the Lord for such wonderful gifts, gifts for the present and for eternity which the human mind cannot measure.

[13]Let you be astonished, you great and small men who revere God! Let you, learned clergymen, heed and consider this! Who was it who called me, fool that I am, from among those who are considered wise, expert in law, powerful in speech and general affairs? He passed over these for me, a mere outcast. He inspired me with fear, reverence and patience to be the one who would if possible serve the people faithfully to whom the love of Christ brought me. The love of Christ indeed gave me to them to serve them humbly and sincerely for my entire lifetime if I am found worthy.

[14]My decision to write must be made, then, in the light of our faith in the Trinity. The gift of God

and his eternal consolation must be made known regardless of danger. I must fearlessly and frankly spread the name of God everywhere in order to leave a legacy after my death to my brothers and children, the many thousands of them, whom I have baptised in the Lord. [15]I was not at all worthy to receive so much grace among these people, after all the trials and difficulties, after captivity and the lapse of so many years. The Lord, indeed, gave much to me, his poor slave, more than as a young man I ever hoped for or even considered.

CHAPTER 2

ESCAPE FROM CAPTIVITY

Morning and night prayers

When[16]I had come to Ireland I tended herds every day and I used to pray many times during the day. More and more my love of God and reverence for him began to increase. My faith grew stronger and my zeal so intense that in the course of a single day I would say as many as a hundred prayers, and almost as many in the night. This I did even when I was in the woods and on the mountains. Even in times of snow or frost or rain I would rise before dawn to pray. I never felt the worse for it; nor was I in any way lazy because, as I now realise, I was full of enthusiasm.

First escape

[17]In my sleep there one night I heard a voice saying to me: "It is well that you fast, soon you will go to your own country." After a short while

I again heard a voice saying: "Look, your ship is ready." It was quite a distance away, about two hundred miles; I never had been to the place, nor did I know anyone there. I ran away and left the man with whom I had spent six years. The power of God directed my way successfully and nothing daunted me until I reached that ship.

[18]The day I arrived the ship was set afloat and I spoke to the boatmen in order that I might be allowed to sail with them. But the captain was annoyed and he retorted angrily: "On no account are you to try to go with us." When I heard this I left them to go back to the hut where I was lodging. On the way I began to pray, and before I had ended my prayer I heard one of them shouting after me: "Come quickly, those men are calling you." I went back to them at once and they began to say to me: "Come on, we will take you under our guarantee; make your bond of friendship with us in any way you wish." Earlier that day I had refused to suck their nipples out of reverence for God, but rather hoped they would allow me to come on the guarantee of Jesus Christ for they were heathens. Thus I now got my way with them and we set sail at once.

[19]After three days we came to land and for twenty-eight days we made our way through deserted country. Supplies ran out and the party was the worse for hunger. The next day the captain said to me: "Tell me this, Christian. You say your God is great and all-powerful; why then can you not pray for us? As you see we are suffering from hunger; it is unlikely indeed that we will

ever see a human being again." I said to them
confidently: "Turn sincerely with your whole
heart to the Lord my God, because nothing is
impossible for him, that this day he may send
you food on your way until you are satisfied; for
he has plenty everywhere." And with the help
of God so it happened. Suddenly a herd of pigs
appeared on the road before our eyes; they killed
many of them and stopped there for two nights.
They were well fed, as were their dogs, and had
their bodies restored to vigour, for many of them
had grown weak and had been left half-dead along
the way. After this they gave profuse thanks to
God and they held me in great esteem. From that
day they had plenty of food. They even found
wild honey and offered me some. One of them
said: "This is offered in sacrifice." Thank God,
from then on I tasted none of it. [22]As well as food
for the journey he also gave us fire and dry weather
every day until we met people ten days later. As
I said above, we were in all twenty-eight days
travelling through deserted country and the night
we met people we had not a pick of food left.
[20]That same night when I was asleep Satan tempted
me with a violence which I will remember as long
as I am in this body. There fell on me as it were
a great rock and I could not stir a limb. How did
it occur to me in my ignorance to call on Elijah?
Meanwhile I saw the sun rising in the sky, and
while I was shouting "Elijah! Elijah!" at the top of
my voice the brilliance of that sun fell suddenly
on me and lifted my depression at once. I believe
that I was sustained by Christ my Lord and that

his Spirit was even then calling out on my behalf.
I hope this is how it will be in my time of trouble,
as he said in the Gospel. *On that day,* the Lord
declares, *it is not you who will be speaking; the
Spirit of your Father will be speaking in you*
(Matt. 10: 20).

Second escape

²¹Many years later I was taken captive again.
On my first night among my captors I received a
divine message which said: "You will be with
them for two months." That is just what happened.
On the sixtieth night the Lord rescued me from
their hands.

CHAPTER 3

HOW PATRICK WAS CALLED

Call of the Irish

On [23]another occasion, a few years later, I was in
Britain with my relatives who had welcomed me
as if I were their son and earnestly begged me that
I should never leave them, especially in view of
all the hardships I had endured. It was there one
night I saw the vision of a man called Victor,
who appeared to have come from Ireland with
an unlimited number of letters. He gave me one
of them and I read the opening words which were:
"The voice of the Irish." As I read the beginning
of the letter I seemed at the same moment to hear
the voice of those who were by the wood of Voclut
which is near the Western Sea. They shouted with
one voice: "We ask you, boy, come and walk once
more among us." I was cut to the very heart and
could read no more, and so I woke up. Thank God,
after many years the Lord answered their cry.

Prayer of the Saviour

[24]Another night — whether in me or beside me I do not know, God knows — I was called very clearly with words which I heard but could not understand, except for the following statement at the end of the prayer: "He who has given up his life for you, he it is who speaks in you." At that I awoke full of joy.

Prayer of the Spirit

[25]On yet another occasion I saw a person praying in me. I was as it seemed inside my body and I heard him over me, that is, over the inner man. There he was, praying with great emotion. All this time I was puzzled as I wondered greatly who could possibly be praying inside me. He spoke, however, at the end of the prayer, saying that he was the Spirit. When I awoke I recalled the words of the apostle: *The Spirit comes to help our inadequacy at prayer. For when we cannot choose words in order to pray properly, the Spirit himself expresses our plea with great emotion in a way that cannot be put into words* (Rom. 8 : 26). Again: *The Lord who is our advocate expresses our plea* (1 Jn. 2 : 1).

Final approval

[26]I was put to the test by a number of my seniors who came to cast up my

sins at me in order to discredit my hard work
as bishop of this mission. On that day indeed the
impulse was overpowering to fall away not only
here and now but forever. But the Lord graciously spared his exile and wanderer and helped
me greatly when I was walked on in this way.
The disgrace and blame I felt, however, were
considerable. I pray God that the occasion may
not be charged against me as a sin.

²⁷After thirty years they discovered against me
a confession which I had made before I became
a deacon. In the anxiety of my troubled mind I
confided to my dearest friend what I had done
in my boyhood one day, in one hour indeed,
because I had not yet overcome my sinful ways.
God knows — I don't — whether I was yet fifteen.
I did not believe in the living God, nor did I
from my childhood, but remained in death and
unbelief until I was severely punished. I was well
and truly reduced by hunger and poor clothing
and every day ²⁸I was in Ireland I had to travel
against my will until I was almost exhausted. All
this was really to my advantage, for as a result I
was purified by the Lord. He prepared me in a
way which has improved me so much from my
former condition that I now care and work for
the salvation of others whereas then I did not
even consider my own.

²⁹The night following my condemnation by
those mentioned above, I had a vision. I was
confronted by the manuscript which dishonoured
me, and simultaneously I heard God's voice saying
to me: "We have seen with disapproval the face

of the chosen one deprived of his good name."
He did not say "you have disapproved" but "we
have disapproved", as if to include himself. As
he says: *He who touches you touches the apple
of my eye* (Zech. 2 : 8). [30]Thanks be to God who
supported me in everything, that he did not
hinder the mission I had undertaken nor the work
I had been given by Christ the Lord. I now felt a
great strength in me and my confidence in
myself was vindicated before God and man. [31]I
say openly that my conscience will always be
clear and God is my witness that I have told no
lies in my account to you.

[32]My only sorrow that we should have deserved
to hear such a report is for my dearest friend. To
him I had confided my very soul. Before my
defence was debated on that occasion I was told
by some of the brothers that he would stand up
for me in my absence. Now I was not there to
hear this myself, nor was I in Britain at the
debate, nor indeed do I propose to bring up the
subject again. He it was who had said to me in
person: "Look, you ought to be raised to the
rank of bishop", although I was unworthy. How
then did it occur to him afterwards to let me
down publicly before all, good and bad, in a
matter in which he had previously favoured me?
For he had done this spontaneously and gladly,
and not he alone but the Lord also who is greater
than all.

[33]Enough said. But I cannot hide the gift of
God which he gave me in the land of my captivity.
There I sought him and there I found him. I am

convinced that he kept me from all evil because
of his Spirit who lives in me and works in me to
this very day. This is a bold claim. But God knows
if a mere man had said this to me it may be that
I would have held my tongue out of Christian
charity.

Prayer of thanksgiving

[34]I give thanks to my God tirelessly who kept
me faithful in the day of trial, so that today I
offer sacrifice to him confidently, the living sacrifice
of my life to Christ, my Lord, who preserved me
in all my troubles. I can say therefore: Who am I,
Lord, and what is my calling that you should
cooperate with me with such divine power?
Today, among heathen peoples, I praise and proclaim your name in all places, not only when things
go well but also in times of stress. Whether I
receive good or ill, I return thanks equally to God,
who taught me always to trust him unreservedly.
His answer to my prayer inspired me in these
latter days to undertake this holy and wonderful
work in spite of my ignorance, and to imitate in
some way those who, as the Lord foretold, would
preach his Good News as a witness to all nations
before the end of the world. We saw it that way
and it happened that way. We are indeed witnesses
that the Good News has been preached in distant
parts, in places beyond which no man lives.

CHAPTER 4

MISSION TO THE IRISH

Success due to God

Now [35]it would be tedious to give a detailed account of all my labours or even a part of them. Let me tell you briefly how the merciful God often freed me from slavery; how he rescued me twelve times when my life was in danger, as well as from numerous conspiracies which I cannot recount. I do not wish to bore my readers; but God, who knows all things in advance, is my witness that he used to forewarn me often by a divine message, poor orphan and all as I am.

[36]How did I come by this wisdom which was not my own, I who neither knew what was in store for me, nor what it was to relish God? What was the source of the gift I got later, the great and beneficial gift of knowing and loving God, even if it meant leaving my homeland and my relatives?

[37]Many gifts were offered to me in sorrow and tears. I offended the donors and went against the wishes of some of my seniors. Under

the guidance of God I neither agreed with them
nor yielded to their objections. It was overpowering grace in me and no virtue of my own
which resisted them all. I came to the Irish
heathens to preach the Good News and to put
up with insults from unbelievers. I heard my
mission abused, I endured many persecutions
even to the extent of chains; I gave up my free-
born status for the good of others. Should I be
worthy I am ready to give even my life, promptly
and gladly, for his name; and it is there that I
wish to spend it until I die, if the Lord should
graciously allow me.

[38]I am very much in debt to God, who gave
me so much grace that through me many people
were born again in God and afterwards confirmed,
and that clergy were ordained for them everywhere. All this was for a people newly come to
belief whom the Lord took from the very ends
of the earth as he promised long ago, through his
prophets: *To you the nations will come from
the ends of the earth and will say "How false are
the idols our fathers made for themselves, how
useless they are"* (Jer.16:19). And again: *I have
made you a light for the nations so that you may
be a means of salvation to the ends of the earth*
(Acts 13 : 47).

Duty to preach the Gospel

[39]I wish to wait there for the promise of one
who never breaks his word, as he promises in the
Gospel: *They will come from the east and the*

west to take their places with Abraham and Isaac
and Jacob (Matt. 8 : 11), just as we believe the
faithful will come from every part of the world.
[40]For that reason we ought to fish well and
diligently in accordance with the advice and
teaching of the Lord, who says: *Follow me and I
will make you fishers of men* (Matt. 4 : 19). There
are also the words of the prophets: *Look, says
God, I am sending many fishermen and many
huntsmen* (Jer. 16 : 16), and so on.

It was then most necessary to spread out our
nets so that a very great multitude might be
caught for God and that there might be clergy
everywhere to baptise and preach to a people in
need and want. As the Lord says in the Gospel
by way of exhorting and teaching: *Go therefore,
teach all the nations, baptise them in the name
of the Father and of the Son and of the Holy
Spirit, teach them to observe all the commands I
gave you. Know that I am with you always, even
to the end of time* (Matt. 28 : 19). Again he
says: *Go out to the whole world and proclaim
the Good News to all creation. He who believes
and is baptised will be saved; he who does not
believe will be condemned* (Mark 16 : 15). And
again: *This Good News of the Kingdom will be
proclaimed to the whole world as a witness to
all the nations. And then the end will come*
(Matt. 24 : 14).

In the same way the Lord predicts through the
prophet: *In the days to come — it is the Lord who
speaks — I will pour out my spirit on all mankind.
Your sons and daughters will prophesy, your young*

men will see visions, your old men will dream
dreams. Even on my slaves, men and women, I
will pour out my spirit in those days, and they
will prophesy (Acts 2:17). In Hosea he says:
I shall say to a people that was not mine, "You
are my people", and to a nation I never pitied,
"I pity you". Instead of being told, "You are no
people of mine", they will be called the sons of
the living God (Rom.9 : 25).

Fervour of Irish converts

[41]How, then, does it happen that in Ireland a
people who in their ignorance of God always
worshipped idols and unclean things in the past,
have now become a people of the Lord and are
called children of God? How is it that the sons
and daughters of Irish chieftains are seen to be
monks and virgins dedicated to Christ?

[42]There was, in particular, a virtuous Irish lady
of noble birth and great beauty, already grown
to womanhood. I had baptised her myself. A few
days later she came to us with a problem on her
mind. She had been advised, in a divine message,
she said, to become a nun and thus to approach
more nearly to God. Thanks be to God, six days
later she carried out what he had proposed and
dedicated herself with a fine enthusiasm to God.
So, too, the other virgins. Their fathers disapprove
of them, so they often suffer persecution and
unfair abuse from their parents; yet their number
goes on increasing. Indeed, the number of

virgins from our converts is beyond counting,
and to these must be added the widows and those
who forego their marriage rights. Of them all the
women who live in slavery suffer the most. They
have to endure terror and threats all the time.
But the Lord gives grace to many of his handmaids and, although they are forbidden, they
follow him courageously.

Human problems

⁴³It is not practical for me to consider leaving
them and going to Britain. How dearly would I
love to go, like a man going to his homeland and
relatives, and not only there but also to Gaul in
order to visit the brothers and to meet the
members of the Christian community! God knows
how I yearned for it, but I am tied by the Spirit.
He has made it clear to me that if I were to do
this he would hold me responsible and I am afraid
of undoing the work which I have begun. It was
not really I who began it but Christ the Lord who
told me to come here and to stay with them for
the rest of my life. The Lord willing, he will
protect me from everything that is evil so that I
may commit no sin against him.
⁴⁴This, I take it, is my duty, but I do not trust
myself as long as I am in this mortal body. Strong
is the enemy who tries every day to turn me
away from the faith and purity of that true
religion to which I have devoted myself to the
end of my life for Christ my Lord. My uncooperative
body is forever dragging me towards death, that

is, towards the satisfaction of unlawful desires,
and I realise that I did not altogether lead a life
as perfect as other believers. But I confess it to
my Lord and I do not blush in his sight because
I am not telling lies. From the time in my early
manhood when I came to know him, the love of
God and reverence for him have grown in me,
and up to now, by the favour of God, I have kept
the faith.

⁴⁵Let him who wishes laugh and scoff. I do not
intend to be silent, nor to conceal the signs and
wonders which the Lord showed me many years
before they happened, as befits him who knew
everything, even before the beginning of time.
⁴⁶I must return unending thanks to God who often
pardoned my folly and my carelessness, and on
more than one occasion spared me his great wrath.
Although he chose me to be his helper I was slow
to accept the prompting of the Spirit. The Lord
showed kindness to me a million times because
he saw that I was ready, even if I did not know
what to do about my position because of the
number of people who were blocking my mission.
They used to discuss me among themselves behind
my back: "Why does this fellow throw himself
into danger among enemies who have no knowledge of God?" There was no malice on their part;
they simply did not appreciate how my mission
should be regarded on account of my lack of
education, and I freely admit this myself. I failed
myself to realise in good time the grace that was
then in me. It is obvious to me now what I should
have understood earlier.

[47]Now I have given here a simple account to my brothers and fellow-captives. They entrusted themselves to me because of what I foretold and still foretell in order to strengthen and consolidate your faith. Would that you, too, would reach out to greater things and do better! This will be my happiness, for *a wise son is the honour of his father* (Prov. 10 : 1).

Money matters

[48]You know, as does God, how I have behaved among you from my early manhood, with genuine faith and a sincere heart. I have equally kept faith with the heathens among whom I live and I do not intend to let them down now. God knows I have exploited none of them for the sake of God and his Church; the mere thought would not occur to me. I would be afraid of provoking persecution against them and against us all, or that through me the name of the Lord would be blasphemed. It is written: *Woe betide the man who causes the name of the Lord to be blasphemed* (Matt. 18: 7).

[49]Although I am unskilled in every way I have tried somehow to avoid being spoiled by my Christian brothers, and by the nuns and the devout women who used to offer me little presents unasked and would even leave some of their jewellery on the altar. When I insisted on giving them back they were offended. But mine was the long-term view and for that reason I used take every

precaution so that the heathen might not catch
me out on any issue concerning myself or
the work of my ministry. I was unwilling to give
unbelievers even the slightest opportunity of
slander or disparagement. [50]In the many thousands
of baptisms which I performed, did I ever take
even a penny from anyone? Tell me and I will give
it back. Or when the Lord ordained through my
unworthy person so many clergy and gave them
spiritual office, did I ever ask of any of them
even the price of a pair of shoes? Speak up and I
will return it.

[51]On the contrary, I spent money in your
interest that I might be accepted; I travelled
among you and on your account exposed myself
to many dangers everywhere, even in the most
remote districts beyond which no man lives and
where nobody had ever come to baptise, to ordain
clergy or to confirm the people. It was the Lord's
gift to me that I undertook everything with
concern and eagerness for your salvation. [52]All
the while I used to give presents to the kings over
and above the expenses I paid their sons who
travel with me. Even so they attacked my companions and me once and were fanatically bent
on killing me that day; but my time had not yet
come. They made off with everything they got
their hands on and put me in chains. Fourteen
days later the Lord rescued me from their power
and our belongings were returned through the
offices of God and the good friends we had made
previously. [53]You have had experience also of
how much I paid the brehons in all the districts

which I used to visit very often. I must have distributed not less than the price of fifteen men among them in order that you might have the pleasure of my company and that I might always have the pleasure of yours until we·meet God. I do not regret this; I do not consider it enough. I am still spending and will go on spending more. The Lord has power to allow me ultimately to spend myself in the interest of your souls.

Purity of motive

[54]Look, I call upon God to witness by my life that I am not telling lies; that neither am I writing to you out of flattery or greed for money, nor because I look for esteem from any of you. Sufficient is the esteem which is not yet seen but which is felt in the heart. Faithful is he who made the promise; he never tells a lie. [55]I see that even in this world I have been exalted beyond measure by the Lord. Now I was neither worthy of this nor a likely choice for the privilege.

I know perfectly well that poverty and misfortune suit me better than riches and pleasure. Christ the Lord, himself, was poor for our sakes, and I am myself in dire straits. Even if I wished for it I have no wealth; nor do I pass judgement on myself in this matter, for I daily expect to be murdered or robbed or reduced to slavery in one way or another. Not‘that I fear any of these things. Because of his promises I leave myself in the hands of almighty God who rules everywhere. As the prophet says: *Unload your burden on the Lord and he will support you.* (Ps. 55 : 22).

Prayer for perseverance

[56]I now entrust my soul to God, who is most faithful and for whom I am an ambassador in my humble station. For God has no favourites and he chose me for this office to become one of his ministers, even if among the least of them.

[57]What return can I make to him for all his goodness to me? What can I say or what can I promise to my Lord since any ability I have comes from him? Suffice it for him to look into my heart and mind; for I am ready and indeed greatly desire it that he should give me his cup to drink, as he gave it to others who loved him. [58]My only prayer to God is that it may never happen that I should leave his people which he won for himself at the end of the earth. I ask God for perseverance, to grant that I remain a faithful witness to him for his own sake until my passing from this life.

[59]If I ever did anything worth doing for my God, whom I love, I beg of him the grace to shed my blood while still with those who are also exiles and captives on his account. Though I should be denied a grave, though my corpse should be utterly torn to pieces and scattered to dogs and wild animals, though the birds of the air should devour it; I would be fully confident in this event that I had saved both body and soul. For on that

day we will undoubtedly rise in the brightness of the sun, that is, in the glory of Christ Jesus our Redeemer, as sons of the living God, joint heirs with Christ and made in his image. From him and through him and for him we will reign. [60]This sun which we see rises daily at his command for our benefit, but it will never reign, nor will its brilliance endure. Those who worship it will be severely punished. We, on the other hand, believe in and worship Christ the true sun who will never perish, nor will anyone who does his will. He will remain for ever as Christ remains for ever, who reigns with God the Father Almighty and the Holy Spirit before time began and now and for all eternity. Amen.

CONCLUSION

Briefly

Look, [61]I wish to explain briefly the words of my confession again and again. Before God and his holy angels I solemnly and gladly swear that I had never any motive other than the Gospel and his promises to go back to that nation from which previously I had only barely escaped.

A final request
[62]A request of those who believe, and revere God. If any of you see fit to examine or to obtain this document, which has been written in Ireland by Patrick an uneducated sinner, do not attribute to me in my ignorance the little I achieved or pointed out which pleased God. Let your conclusion and the general opinion rather be the real truth, that my success was the gift of God.

This is my confession before I die.

See notes on the *Confession*, Appendix Two, page 98.

PART TWO: ROOTS OF A PERSONALITY

CHAPTER 1

RICHES TO RAGS

St Patrick's cultural identity can best be summed up by the simple statement that he was a Roman citizen. Like the founder and first apostles of his faith he was born into a world which centred on Rome and which was dominated by the Roman way of life. During those first four centuries of the Christian era there had been further political expansion and constant dynastic changes. But the Empire never quite regained the extraordinary vigour and stability of the reign of Augustus. One of the many reform measures had been to divide the administration into East and West, a division which in time hardened both politically and culturally. The western half in 379 contained the Pretorian Prefectures of Italy and the Gauls, in other words the dioceses of Italy, Rome, Africa, Gaul (France), Spain and Britain. For a few months in 395 the great emperor Theodosius managed to unite both halves but he was the last man ever to rule the Roman Empire as an effective unit.

The initiative in Europe had long passed from

the Romans to the different peoples who lived to
the north and east of the Empire. Time and again
they advanced, Goths, Vandals, Franks, Saxons,
Picts and Scots. Before Theodosius their incursions
had at least been controlled, and efforts had been
made with some success to assimilate them, to the
extent of sharing power with them. When he died the
situation soon got completely out of hand. A
great Vandal raid devastated Gaul in 407. In
410, on August 23 Alaric and his Goths swept into
Rome itself and sacked the city for three days.
News of these sensational happenings must have
reached the home of Patrick who lived within
easy access of the seafaring invaders of the north-
west. The conversation of his parents must have
reflected the general dismay and consternation.
Where would the barbarian find his next target?

Disaster struck suddenly and violently. Patrick's
home was attacked, his father's servants cruelly
butchered and the boy taken off with many others
as a slave to Ireland. At this crisis-point in his life
— he was then sixteen — we can get some idea of
the world he was leaving behind him. He had been
enjoying his boyhood life to the full, with all the
privileges and self-assurance of a well-off and
respected family. His father was a deacon in the
local church; he was also a *decurio* or member of
the municipal council. He was therefore in the
mainstream of communications and had all the
loyalty of a civil servant to imperial institutions.
The Roman way of life was not only the social
fabric of a long and rooted tradition; it was the
only life-style which Patrick's family knew. In

spite of all the upheavals Patrick himself was
genuinely proud of his freeborn citizenship of
the Empire and remained a fervent Roman to the
end of his days.

Like any young Roman Patrick went to school.
He attended first a *ludus* where reading, writing
and arithmetic were taught by the *ludi magister*.
He then went to the *grammaticus* who concentrated
on a more critical knowledge of the Latin language
and prepared boys for the *rhetor*. Patrick unfortunately
never reached the *rhetor.* and therefore missed a
training in Latin composition and oratory which
would have completed his general education. This
proved to be a severe handicap in later life and
caused him acute embarrassment and distress. It
also obscured in his writings the natural brilliance
of his lively mind and the depth and range of his
emotions.

In sharp contrast to his hypersensitivity about
his unfinished literary education, Patrick describes
his early religious outlook rather disarmingly:
"We neither kept his commandments nor obeyed
our pastors who used to warn us about our
salvation." It is noteworthy that he found no
fault with his religious instruction. Being the son
of a deacon and the grandson of a priest we can
be confident that he was taught his Christian
doctrine more thoroughly than the majority of
his companions. We can also conclude that
Christianity was at least three generations old in
his family.

Throughout the fourth century churches were
established in the cities of Gaul and Britain. In

this way the Church became an integral part of
the Roman establishment, a development which
had obvious effects on the style of religious
practice. Nora Chadwick[1] has written of a fifth-
century bishop, Sidonius Apollinaris, that his
letters and poems "charming and personal and
intimate as they are, convey rather the impression
of an official ecclesiastic than of a man with
deep inner religious life and vision". Yet we know
that many bishops of the time often went
outside their routine duties and gave generously
of their personal store to those in need. In short,
they reflected the image of decent conformity,
the uneven blend of active responsibility and
passive sobriety which normally distinguishes
any group of churchmen whose lives settle into
a regular pattern.

The stimulant — and the discord — within the
Western Church at this time was provided by the
advent of spiritual asceticism from the East.
From Egypt and Syria came news of the Desert
Fathers and their heroic and often eccentric
ideals of austerity and contemplation. Patrick
was too fond of life and fun to take seriously
to asceticism while he was still at home, but it is
understandable that his religious practice should
have taken this turn when he found himself in
Ireland away from the Sacraments and organised
Church life. He gradually adapted to the spiritual
needs of his isolated situation the habits of those
like Martin of Tours and Germanus of Auxerre
who sought out caves and wooden cells wherein

1. The Celtic Realms (London 1967), 164

to praise God, while living full and busy lives in the daily round of general affairs.

Perhaps the most vivid symbol of Patrick's background was the *toga*, the loose-fitting cloak which was the characteristic garment of the Roman citizen. By the fifth century the *toga* had long since been superseded in ordinary life by more manageable forms of dress, but it retained a ceremonial use until the end of the Empire and could only be worn by the freeborn citizen. In Ireland Patrick had to exchange his fine clothes for the rags and cast-offs of his captors, and had to endure a humiliation which was nothing less than a personal catastrophe. Many years later when he returned to the land of his captivity his outlook on life had changed radically. He was now happy to sacrifice the external trappings of his Roman status for the opportunity he got to transmit the more personal and more valuable part of his heritage, his Christian faith and religion.

CHAPTER 2

THE HUMAN TOUCH

Patrick was blessed with a strong and robust constitution. After twenty-eight days in the desert he was still on his feet when many of his companions were lying half-dead along the way. His early experience of roughing it does not seem to have come against him in later life. His powers of endurance, physical courage and boundless energy remind one forcibly of St Paul who was also subjected to continual hardship and danger.

Like Paul, Patrick was a born orator, a thoroughly convincing preacher who spoke straight from the heart and who made instant contact with his audience. His language was the plain and rural speech of the Irish which he had picked up in captivity and which had to be moulded personally by Patrick to express the basic concepts of a new religion. He left to his successors the task of teaching Latin to the Irish and of adapting the finer shades of Graeco-Latin theology to the native tongue. Patrick's style was rather that of the storyteller who relishes concrete rather than

abstract language, who prefers the emotional and
familiar to the formal and clinical, who has the
knack of recalling the trivial detail which gives
a conversation colour and life. The point has been
well taken by the late Donnchadh Ó Floinn[2] :
"How his unbookish common sense must have
baffled those suave and contriving learned
opponents of his! And how his broad sympathy
must have won over those rugged though kindly
ancestors of ours, whose generosity was excited
by the simple trustfulness of his appeal."

As a leader Patrick's flair was a combination
of enterprise and control. He not merely baptised
a multitude of Irish but ordained clergy for them
and organised their churches. He was forever on
the road, addressing public meetings, interviewing
local princes and brehons (as the Irish judges were
called), encouraging his youthful converts,
arranging sites for new churches, outwitting the
pagan priests or druids who clung to their old
ways with all the native conservatism of the Irish,
and who saw in Patrick's retinue a threat to be
destroyed. It has often been noted that his revolut-
ion is the only bloodless one in the turbulent
history of Ireland. The later compilers of saints'
lives, who were by no means given to understate-
ment, tell of only one martyr in his entire missionary career.

For all his talent in communications and
management and public relations, Patrick had to
cope all his life with a very difficult temperament.
He was at heart a very lonely man with a per-
manent feeling of being isolated and unwanted.

2. *Furrow*(March 1953),137.

There were obvious reasons for this in his own experience. He had no friends to tide him over the storms and special problems of adolescence; he was forced to accept the harsh drudgery of manual work for which he had neither liking nor aptitude; he was later treated callously and very unfairly by those who should have known better, his fellow-clerics. Yet he managed to avoid despair and disillusionment. His way with young people, inspiring a response which amounted to hero-worship on their part, was very likely due to a special concern to give them what had been missing in his own early life.

The young men who travelled around with him and who came to know him intimately must also have learned to recognise his moods. The full blaze of his fury appears only once in print, directed against the soldiers of Coroticus who took the innocent lives of some of his converts. The controlling of such a vast reservoir of emotion was a constant problem, but there was a bright side too. Note the hint of dry humour in the biblical reference early in the *Confession* to the "great and small men who revere God"; the particular mildness and courtesy of his attitude to women matched by an amusing determination not to let them "mother" him.

Apart from the impact of the Christian faith on his life the overwhelming impression we get of Patrick from the *Confession* is one of complete honesty, of a man who has nothing to hide and who sees his vocation in life as bigger than himself. It is rare that a man can talk about himself in this

intimate way with such truth and dignity, and
without appearing in the slightest way conceited.
There is no glossing over embarrassing situations,
no attempt to be merely impressive, in fact no
censorship at all. He had to find his feet in life
without the props of home and family, yet his
years of captivity made a man of him, a man
with a growing sense of a special vocation and
an independent outlook on life. He always found
it very difficult to make up his mind about important problems, like the timing of his escape or the
degree of self-assertion required to launch his
mission, but once the decision was made there
was no turning back. A shrewd practical instinct
made him wary of his own intuitions; he
disciplined his body, and awaited his opportunities
with patience. In a more speculative mood, in
more sustained and profound reflection, he finally
succeeded in seeing beyond the horizon of his
native culture and environment. He slowly and pain-
fully learned the truth of his uniqueness as a
person and of the value of his life in the destiny
of a people, and indeed in the ultimate destiny of
mankind.

CHAPTER 3

MAN WITH A MESSAGE

Patrick's religious views took shape largely in the
Christian community into which he was born. After
captivity he undoubtedly expanded and even
changed his attitude towards various aspects of
doctrine and ritual when he had an opportunity
to travel and visit other churches. But there is
nothing in his writings to suggest that he developed
any eccentric notions, that he veered away at any
point from the interpretation of the New Testament which was generally accepted by the Church
of the fifth century. He stresses more than once
that he had no formal training in theology or law
and he was certainly not a man to get embroiled
in academic controversies. Nevertheless he was
compelled to come to terms with the strong
current of Pelagianism which overflowed into the
pastoral life of the British Church of his day.

The Pelagians claimed in varying degrees that
man could reach his eternal reward without
divine help, and that total reliance on God's grace
merely condoned failure to develop the natural

virtues. Hence their devaluation of Patrick's
missionary vocation at the practical level and
their contempt for his lack of learning. Two other
points of contact with the Church at large keep
Patrick firmly in line with the broader and more
central continental tradition: his profession of
faith in the Trinity which, according to modern
scholars, derives mainly from Victorinus of Pettau,
a late third-century martyr-bishop of the Balkans,
and his use of St Jerome's revision of the New
Testament which was then a very recent work.
Patrick's references to baptism, confirmation and
ordination of clergy are of a very general kind
and could apply to Sacramental practice at any
period of the Church's history.

It was the intensity of Patrick's faith on the
other hand, the strictly personal aspect of it,
which was so remarkable. About the age when a
young man becomes aware and critical of his
own identity, when he begins to look forward
and to plan his future, Patrick came to appreciate
for the first time the religion of his home and
childhood. A truly spiritual and yet personal
relationship with God entered his life. This was
nothing less than a thrilling new way of looking
at the whole mystery of human existence, an
absorbing and enriching ideal which made
unceasing demands on his mind and energy and
gave him a deep inner peace of mind which he
never lost.

Patrick looks back on all this with the
experienced and slightly nostalgic eye of an old
man. His sense of God's love for him was much

more than the compensation of his vivid
imagination for his lost parents; it was a positive
gift which mysteriously reached into his heart, a
gift which he felt he in no way deserved. He
came to love God because he realised more and
more how God loved him first. The very thought
of what God had done for him moves him to
spontaneous and lyrical prayer. More than once
he remarks that he received this gift in the pain
and loneliness of captivity in a foreign land. His
carefree and self-sufficient world had been
shattered and, even though he felt the loss terribly,
he knew that his early years had been too super-
ficial and without challenge.

In his prayer on the mountain the complete
absence of strain and worry is psychologically
important. The discomfort of wet cold mornings
and the hazards to physical health were real
and unpleasant, but they were at once forgotten
in the excitement and obvious enjoyment of a
man discovering his talent. It was quite otherwise
with the general degradation and menial work as
a slave labourer and herdsboy; Patrick bitterly
resented the injustice of his situation and hated
every minute of it.

The most far-reaching influence and most
profound source of motivation in the miracle of
Patrick's prayer was his faith in the presence of
the Spirit, the third person of the Trinity. Patrick
could point to definite occasions when the
reality of this presence showed itself clearly in
his life and work. It was the Spirit, for example,
who persuaded him not to leave Ireland even

though he felt like the occasional holiday in
Britain and Gaul. It was the Spirit who "called
out on his behalf" in a particularly severe bout
of depression, in other words who put words on
his sentiments and thus enabled him to express himself in a fitting way in order to shake off the attack.
In another dream sequence the Spirit went further
and supplied the sentiments as well. This was a
very special privilege and so extraordinary that
Patrick was baffled by it until he recalled a
similar experience of St Paul, described in his
letter to the Romans.

The insights of Patrick's prayer and meditation
inevitably led him to active service, to pass on the
gift of God that others might also believe. His
model and pattern here was that of all Christians,
the magnetic personality of the Son of God.
Patrick had pledged his loyalty and commitment
to Christ even before he finally escaped from
Ireland. His mission in Ireland was work for Christ,
whom he loved sincerely and who told him to go
there. Similarly, his utter unconcern for personal
material gain and physical security were in
imitation of Christ's own human life. On the last
day, which Patrick, significantly, believed was
imminent, we must appear before Christ and be
judged by him. Those who remain faithful will
share his company for ever because he has
redeemed human kind.

Patrick drops his terse concentrated style only
once in the entire *Confession,* when he comes to
explain his solemn duty to preach the Gospel. He
is at pains to collect and quote in full all the

texts he can to prove his thesis that this obligation is an integral part of the Christian life as he sees it. Note that the Good News is intended for all men without exception. Patrick broke new ground in carrying the Christian message to whole regions of a country outside the Roman Empire. His critics in Britain had no real faith in the project; they despised Patrick for wasting his time among dangerous and treacherous heathens, and they also considered him a financial nuisance.

Patrick, on the other hand, was not merely concerned to travel to every "back of beyond"; his converts ranged over the whole social scale from prince to slavegirl. The spiritual effectiveness of his preaching is most evident from the number of younger converts who not only accepted baptism but dedicated their lives completely to the following of Christ. Patrick himself regarded martyrdom as the ultimate reward, the final proof of his overwhelming desire to share the Passion and death of the Saviour.

PART THREE: BEHIND THE LEGEND

CHAPTER 1

A SHORT BIOGRAPHY

As we have already noted in our introduction to
the *Confession* , modern writers on St Patrick
have warned us of the extreme difficulty of giving
the Saint precise dates and places. Fortunately the
details of historical interpretation are not essential
to the spiritual value of the *Confession,* and their
vagueness and ambiguity must not be allowed to
obscure the general picture which the author
gives of his life and mission.

At the same time, in any version of Patrick's
work, however popular, the sequence and setting
of his career cannot be ignored. One simply
cannot present Patrick without giving him some
definite anchorage in time and place. The
following short biography then is necessarily
subjective and speculative and invites the reader
to search for clues himself in a problem which
has all the fascination of an unsolved mystery.

Patrick was born about 400 A.D. into an
upper-class family of the dwindling and harassed
Roman colony of southern Britain. His father
seems to have left home and to have settled as a

church and civil official in the port of Bononia,
now Boulogne-sur-mer on the French side of the
English channel. Patrick's boyhood language
would therefore have been the unpolished vulgar
Latin of northern Gaul which differed only
marginally from the dialect of Britain where he
later lived.

At the age of sixteen he was captured near
Boulogne by the kinsmen of Niall of the Nine
Hostages, the most powerful ruler of his time
in Ireland and a seafaring warrior himself who is
said to have been killed in the same area.

Patrick was brought with thousands of others
to Niall's political homeland in North Connacht
where he later saw his captors in a dream. The
boy was sold to an Antrim farmer and tended
herds on Slemish mountain for six years.
He then escaped to the south of Ireland where
he boarded a boat which carried a cargo of
dogs and which landed at a deserted port on
the west coast of Gaul. This three-day journey
by sea reminds us that the speed of boats in
those days depended entirely on the supporting
wind; we know for example from the Acts of
the Apostles that St Paul sailed over 150 miles
in one day on his way to Rome.

About 416 we have vivid eye witness descriptions
of the widespread desolation in Gaul which still
prevailed from the invasions of 407-409; this
was followed in the 420s by a civil war between
the Roman Gauls under Aetius and the Visigoths
who overran the country from Italy to the Bay
of Biscay. Hence the 28-day journey through the

wilderness and a likely context for the saying attributed to Patrick in the Book of Armagh: "I had the fear of God as my guide through Gaul and Italy and as far as the Islands of the Tyrrhenian Sea." After many unrecorded adventures and hospitality in many religious houses Patrick returned to his wrecked home at Boulogne but proceeded to his relatives in Britain who received him as one of their own.

He was here a few years later when his first midnight call came from the Irish, a subconscious echo of the visit of Germanus bishop of Auxerre in central Gaul to Britain in 429, which resulted among other more pressing matters in the Papal-sponsored mission of Palladius to Ireland in 431. With the aid of friendly local clergy Patrick saw Germanus, convinced him of the reality of his vocation and went to Auxerre, to the island monastery on the river Yonne where Germanus lived. At the earliest opportunity he was ordained deacon and then bishop, presumably when news came of the death of Palladius. Germanus understood Patrick's special difficulties as a late vocation, recognised his sanctity and missionary potential and no doubt reflected that he had himself been ordained bishop directly from the lay state in 418.

There is no need then to reject entirely the commonly accepted tradition that Patrick set out from Auxerre in 432 to convert the Irish. But his mission was far from being the instant triumphal success imagined by later biographers. For a start he had to make arrangements with the British

bishops who would actually finance his mission
as they did that of Palladius; secondly, he lacked
the fifth-century equivalents of secondary
education, and what was a bigger handicap,
formal training in theology. A mere crash course
even at Auxerre was an unimpressive substitute
for the diplomatic record of Palladius. Thirdly,
the Irish at this period and with good reason were
greatly feared and very unpopular in Roman
Britain; the fate of Patrick's household at their
hands and the mysterious disappearance of
Palladius in their midst were too close for
comfort.

Patrick, of course, had his influential contacts
and ready volunteers, but some of the bishops,
who were of course all older than he, thought his
enterprise foolish and against his own interests,
as did his lay friends. His rapid elevation to
episcopal rank provoked resentment among others;
his obvious lack of learning invited ridicule and
embarrassed him acutely. Frustrated at every turn
he began to distrust his own competence and to
believe his critics.

Uneasy months passed into uneventful years,
but as he settled to live respectably among his
relatives and to make his own of his Latin Bible
the call of the Irish was forever ringing in his
ears. After a delay, possibly of as much as eight
or ten years, which he later regretted and blamed
himself for, he finally asserted himself, gathered
his assistants and sailed for Ireland.

Four or five years later came the great crisis of
Patrick's life, the famous *temptatio*. Germanus

was returning to Britain about 445 for another
review of the heresies and irregularities of the
British Church. He knew he would be called on
to defend his recommendation of Patrick for the
Irish mission, and before leaving for Britain he
publicly announced his intention of supporting
Patrick. His powers, however, were failing — he
died shortly afterwards — and as he lapsed into
reminiscence about his *protégé* he mentioned to
the assembled bishops, perhaps inadvertently
or to prove some point in his argument, a boyhood misdemeanour which Patrick had confessed
at Auxerre. Patrick's enemies in the audience
were jubilant, they had a copy made of the proceed-
ings and hastened to Ireland to bully the
unfortunate Patrick into resigning his mission.
The confrontation almost broke the saint's
morale. Then, in his hour of need and humiliation,
he received unexpected vindication in a dream
and continued his labours with renewed peace
of mind and heart.

From this point Patrick's ministry was an outstanding success and continued for at least a
further thirty years. He never left Ireland and had
many of the same assistants towards the end of
his active life when he wrote the *Confession*. The
most accurate information about his journeys
comes from the seventh-century biographer
Tíreachán who set out to make a list of the
churches which were claimed to have been
founded by Patrick. Tíreachán's findings would
locate Patrick's work mainly in north-east,
central and western Ireland, in an area bounded

roughly by Slemish in Antrim, the scene of his
captivity, and north Mayo where he originally
landed in Ireland.

Patrick's unselfish motives and peculiar
missionary methods were never really understood
by his critics in Britain, who had no experience
of the extra-imperial culture and society of the
Irish, a society which still baffled the invaders of
Gaelic Ireland at the end of the sixteenth century.
In particular, his practice of generosity to win
prestige among chieftains and brehons gave rise
to slanders in Britain that he was encouraging
gifts and money for himself. He incurred further
opprobrium when he vigorously denounced the
soldiers of the Welsh prince Coroticus who had
plundered and murdered some of his converts.

Above all, Patrick identified fully with his Irish
flock in sharing their life and in feeling for their
problems. It is interesting to note that his knowledge of Latin had so far deteriorated through lack
of use that he speaks of turning the Coroticus
letter into Latin and that when he came to write
the *Confession* he needed his Latin Bible for basic
vocabulary. His brief stay in Auxerre had
convinced him of the value of dedicated religious
life but he could never have foreseen the extraordinary expansion of the monastic idea which
was later accepted by his converts. We have no
reliable date for his death but it would be reason-
able to assume that his active life was over about
the year 480.

CHAPTER 2

A TOUR OF THE SITES

The early biographers of Patrick were very liberal
with their association of places with the saint.
Literally hundreds of places were called after
Patrick as devotion to him expanded in the seventh
century in Ireland and spread with the Irish monks
in Britain and on the Continent. One need only
page through the two large volumes of Whitley
Stokes' *The Tripartite Life of Patrick and other
documents relating to that Saint* (London 1887),
or chapter 36 of Louis Gougaud's *Les Saints
Irlandais hors d'Irlande* (Louvain and Oxford
1936), to appreciate at least the geographical
extent to which Patrick won the hearts of the
Irish. St Patrick's Cathedral in New York,
commissioned by Tyrone man Archbishop Hughes,
and St Patrick's Missionary Society, Kiltegan,
are only two examples of modern devotion to
the saint which continues a long tradition going
back to the fifth century. In the *Confession* itself
there are in fact only two places mentioned,
Bannaven Taberniae and Silva Vocluti, and there

has been considerable doubt as to their exact location. Similarly, the other places which maintain a special relationship with the saint can be reduced to a short, if selective, list: Armagh, Auxerre, Croagh Patrick, Downpatrick and Saul, Glaston-bury, Hohenstadt, Lough Derg and Slemish.

ARMAGH

It has been generally agreed that the author of the *Confession* founded his chief church on the hill of Armagh, the site of a pagan shrine two miles from the fortress of the Ulster kings at Eamhain, now Navan Fort. Since O'Rahilly published his famous "Palladius and Patrick" lecture in 1942 scholars have subjected the claims of Armagh to searching and intensive criticism. They have made the point that the seventh-century biographies of Patrick were words of propaganda with the purpose of furthering the interest of the Armagh church and the ruling dynasty of the Uí Néill who controlled it. However, the most recent paper on the subject, "The Aggrandisement of Armagh" by Liam de Paor, published in *Historical Studies VIII* (Dublin 1971) reaches the following con-clusion (p. 96):

Sparse as the evidence is for the early period, it leaves little doubt that Armagh, however much its fortunes may have declined with the rise of great monasteries and monastic federations in the sixth and seventh centuries, had always enjoyed, with Patrick, its founder, some recognition of priority.

There is no better qualified guide to show us around Armagh than an tAthair Tomás Ó Fiaich, writing in his own *Seanchas Ardmhacha* (1961-62), p. 126:

The spot where St Patrick built the Church of the Relics, his first foundation in Armagh, can be traced first as a monastery and then as a convent until the dissolution of religious houses in the sixteenth century. Its site can still be pointed out as occupied by the Bank of Ireland in Scotch Street, and thus all those who enter Armagh today by the main road from Newry pass the very spot where St Patrick founded his first church here. The hilltop site where Patrick made his principal foundation is where the Protestant Cathedral now stands. Its ancient name of Druim Saileach remained in use under the English form Sally Hill until comparatively recent times. Originally a fortified enclosure surrounded by double earthen ramparts whose course around the apex of the hill is followed by gently curving streets, it remained exclusively occupied by ecclesiastical buildings and was the nucleus around which the later town of Armagh grew up.

AUXERRE

It used to be taken for granted that Patrick received his clerical education at Auxerre, a diocesan seat in central Gaul about a hundred miles south-east of Paris. Professor Binchy has suggested that Patrick's link with Auxerre derives

from an early confusion of his *acta* with those of
the deacon Palladius who was sent to Ireland in
431. The main difficulty with this hypothesis is
that it cuts Patrick off from the mainstream of
the British church with which Germanus of
Auxerre and Palladius were both closely associated
in 429. It would be highly unlikely that a mission
as extensive and controversial as that headed by
Patrick would have been organised in Britain
independently of Germanus, who seems to have
had a watching brief over the British bishops.
This in itself, of course, would not bring Patrick
to Auxerre but it certainly helps to interpret the
Confession if we give Patrick a minimum stay there.

René Louis in *Seanchas Ardmhacha* (1961-62)
proposed the fascinating theory that the famous
island of Aralanensis where Patrick is said to have
studied was not in the Tyrrhenian Sea as Tíreachán
thought but in the immediate vicinity of Auxerre
itself. From his intimate knowledge of the locality
he is convinced that the monastery of Germanus
on the right bank of the river Yonne included at
least one island in the river and that this is where
Patrick studied.

BANNAVEN TABERNIAE

John Lanigan's identification of this elusive
placename with Bononia and the medieval diocese
of Tarvenna or Tarabanna in north-east Gaul
deserves a fresh inquiry; see his *Ecclesiastical
History of Ireland* (Dublin 1822) i, pp. 92-96. The

similarity of Taberniae and Tarbennae as
manuscript readings is particularly impressive,
especially when we recall the three-century interval
between Patrick's death and the composition of
the Book of Armagh in 807 which contains the
oldest copy of the *Confession*. Later copies have
Taburniae or Thaburniae. Unfortunately for his
theory Lanigan assumed that Patrick was born
here rather than in Wales or England, an assump-
tion which is not demanded by the text of the
Confession. Patrick was certainly of Roman-
British stock and it is very likely that Calpornius
at least was born in Britain where Patrick's
relatives lived.

Bononia, now Boulogne-sur-mer, is still a
favourite and convenient venue for British day-
trippers on a shopping expedition. Even on a
fairly clear day one can see the English coast in
detail from the rocks above the town. We have
here the Portus Itius from which Julius Caesar
sailed for Britain in 54 B.C. In much later times
Napoleon Bonaparte and Adolf Hitler also
thought of invading Britain from here, and only
changed their minds at the last moment.

Tarvenna or Tarabanna is the modern town
of Thérouanne about thirty miles away and much
declined in prestige since it was destroyed by
the emperor Charles V in 1553. The old diocese of
the name, according to an 1813 reference quoted
by Lanigan (p.96), "contained 800 parishes in
the countries of Flanders, Artois and the
Boulonnais". "The Boulonnais" is still used of
the district round Boulogne.

Christine Mohrmann's observations on the
provenance of Patrick's Latin must be mentioned
here. Her discovery in his writings of unbookish
and colloquial contact with the early fifth-century
Latin of northern Gaul is more easily understood
in terms of Patrick's childhood than of a later
extended stay at a Gaulish monastery or
church. See *The Latin of St Patrick* (Dublin 1961),
pp. 21, 47-48.

Lanigan (p. 96) was also able to use an argument from local tradition. This would be quite
worthless in itself but is a necessary support for
any theory which attempts to locate Bannaven
Taberniae.

CROAGH PATRICK

In the Annals of Loch Cé A.D. 1121 we read
that "a thunderbolt fell on Cruachán Aigle in
the night of the festival of Patrick, which destroyed thirty of the fasting people". This is the earliest
reference to *turas na cruaiche,* the pilgrimage to
the Reek which still brings sixty thousand people
to the top of a Mayo mountain on the last Sunday
of July every year.

The Reek is the most obvious example of how
the memory of Patrick worked itself into and
finally penetrated the older pagan mythology
and folklore of the Irish. This was probably a
much slower process than the legends would
imply; indeed a trace of the older cult has
survived in the stories of Crom Dubh. In the

Connacht Gaeltacht the last Sunday of July is
known as Domhnach Chrom Dubh and the stories
tell of Patrick, more in the style of a mediaeval
knight than of a Christian bishop, ousting Crom
in the latter's abode on the mountain. Crom Dubh
is sometimes identified with the more famous
idol, Crom Cruaich, to whom sacrifice was offered
at Samhain (1st November), which was the greatest
feast in the year.

DOWNPATRICK

Knowledge of Patrick's burial place was lost at
an early stage. Scholars agree that the honour
was never claimed by the church of Armagh and
tend to the view that Patrick crossed the Bann
with the defeated Ulstermen when they were
ousted from Eamhain and that he ended his days
in their new shrunken kingdom of Antrim and
Down. At any rate the Norman John de Courcy
claimed in 1183 that the relics of Patrick, Brigid
and Colmcille were in Down where he had
established himself in 1177. He used this pretext
to transfer the diocesan See to Down from the
great monastery of Bangor. About the same time
a famous Life of St Patrick was written here by
Jocelin, a Cistercian monk from Furness in
Lancashire. This was probably the most popular
of all the lives of St Patrick and a Gaelic version
of Jocelin's Latin was still being copied in the
closing years of the 18th century.

Two miles from Downpatrick is Saul where

Patrick is said to have made his first church of
a barn donated by a local chieftain.

GLASTONBURY

   Another "tomb" of St Patrick was discovered
in the old church of St Mary at Glastonbury in
Somerset, England. This church and its anti-
quities were described by William of Malmesbury
who wrote between 1125 and 1130 and has
associations not only with Patrick but also with
Brigid, Benignus and Indract. Excavations in
1891 unearthed a pre-Norman chapel of St Brigid
and there is evidence that many lives of Irish
saints were collected or written there. Pilgrims
flocked here from Ireland all through the Middle
Ages.

HOHENSTADT

   The outstanding shrine of St Patrick in
Continental Europe is at Hohenstadt, near Aalen
in southern Germany, about 70-75 miles north-
west of Munich. Veneration of the saint which
survives today among the farming community
of the district is due to the Adelmann family who
donated a statue of Patrick to the church of the
neighbouring village of Neubronn in the late 14th
century. After the wars of the Reformation the
statue was taken to Hohenstadt in 1652, and
remains there. To accommodate the growing

number of pilgrims a large baroque church was built by Wilhelm von Adelmann in 1711.

The modern annual pilgrimage on 17th March is well described by Gertrude Mesmer in the *Irish Ecclesiastical Record* (March 1959). She quotes the song the people sing in German:

We greet you with praise,
St Patrick, confessor of our Lord,
Thou shepherd, never afraid,
Be not far from us as leader.
Please, accompany us,
Please help us to fight;
St Patrick, guide us,
Thou shining star.

LOUGH DERG

St Patrick's Purgatory in Lough Derg, Co. Donegal, is the only shrine which preserves the living asceticism of an ancient Celtic monastery. About 20,000 pilgrims come here every summer to perform a three-day programme of vocal prayer, fasting and vigil. This island-shrine was widely known all over Europe before the Reformation. The oldest relic on the island, which bore the full fury and devastation of the 17th-century wars, is a mediaeval stone column called St Patrick's Cross. The Basilica (1926-31) also named after the saint, and where pilgrims keep vigil today, is the only church in Ireland or Britain with this title.

The origin of the pilgrimage derives from a cave on the island where pilgrims traditionally kept vigil and which was closed finally as late as 1780. Fortunately a number of Gaelic poems survive which give us a firsthand account of popular devotion to St Patrick here before the destruction of the old way of life in the 17th century. They are the work of the bardic poets, the professional literary craftsmen of the O'Higgins, the O'Dalys, the MacAwards and the Conrys, whose mentality was that of the educated Gaelic ruling class of the later Middle Ages. Their poetry in general was stilted and repetitious but never flippant nor sentimental. Because their ideas and outlook were so similar we can accept them as typical and authentic mouthpieces of their age.

Feargal Og O'Higgin knows exactly why he has come to Lough Derg and what to expect:

Tuig go bhfuil an bás id bhun
Ná bí, a cholann, id chodladh.
Gar uaibh do leabaidh lighe
Freagair uair na haithrighe.

An peacthach truagh bhíos i mbraid
D'éis a luighe i linn Phádraig
Fágbhaidh an sruth sul tí is-teagh
Sa chruth i mbí ar na bhaisteadh.

Do fhágaibh Dia do dhealbh neamh
Do leigheas locht ár sinsear
Pádraig 's an iris do b'fhearr
In inis fhádbhuig Éireann.

Remember that death is busy upon thee; be not drowsy,
O body; thy bed is near; use the time of penance.

The poor enslaved sinner, after lying in Patrick's lake, must
leave the water before he can become as he was after
Baptism.

God, Creator of Heaven, wishing to cure our first parents'
sin, left in soft-grassed Eire Patrick and his splendid guidance.

Donnchadh Mór O'Daly felt that his pilgrimage
had been a waste of time because he was still
unmoved by his sins. He contrasts his mood with
that of Patrick:

> Gan tuirse croidhe gan maoith
> Gan doilgheas ag caoi mo locht
> Níor shaoil Pádraig, ceann na gcliar,
> Go bhfuigheadh sé Dia mar so.

Lamenting my sins, but without heart-sore or sorrow or
brief. Not so did Patrick, chief of clergy, seek God.

For Tadhg Dall O'Higgin Patrick is the great
healer, the surgeon who still binds the wounds of
the Irish, who is "ag síor-chabhair fear nÉireann".
For Tuileagna Mac Torna he is a very powerful
advocate who will help those like the poet who
are desperately in need.

Of the long history of genuine devotion to
Patrick on Lough Derg within the rational frame-
work and sober discipline of Christian teaching
there is no doubt. The same cannot be said of
Patrick's actual physical connection with the
place. The earliest saint associated with the localit
was not Patrick at all but Dabheoc or Davog. It
was not until the 12th century, when Davog's
monastery was taken over by the Canons Regular

of St Augustine, that the legend of St Patrick
and the cave began to circulate. According to
this legend Patrick had been given on Lough
Derg a personal and miraculous glimpse of the
Otherworld where the suffering souls lay in
unspeakable torment. His experience was later
transferred to the Norman knight Owen who
brought the myth of the cave as a superstitious
if glamorous curiosity all over Europe. Philippe
de Félice in his *L'Autre Monde* (Paris 1906)
makes a plausible case for finding the origin of
the cave in pre-Christian mythology and pagan
ideas of life after death. Certainly the theme of
Patrick's experience of Purgatory was a development of Irish vision and voyage literature, exchang-
ing of course the romance of Tír na nÓg for the
horrors of hell.

The strict regulations which governed the
pilgrimage in 1186 point to perhaps the earliest
effort to apply the Christian doctrine of penance
to an already well-established legend and to lift
the ritual above pagan superstition. Unfortunately,
in later centuries, especially after the Reformation,
many visitors to the shrine saw only what appeared to be superstition and missed the genuine
penitential spirit which was always the only
reason why the pilgrimage was officially approved
by the Church.

SILVA VOCLUTI

Dr Mac Philibín in his *Mise Pádraig* (Dublin
1961), pp. 90-91, translates Silva Vocluti as

"Coill Acla" (Achill Wood) and notes that Achill originally applied to a large area of Mayo. This view agrees with the seventh-century Tíreachán, a native of the district, who claimed that the wood was near Killala.

Patrick apparently spent enough time in Mayo as a captive to form first and lasting impressions of the pagan Irish in their native habitat before he was brought to Antrim.

SLEMISH

Both Patrick's seventh-century biographers, Muirchú and Tíreachán, who wrote independently of each other, identified the site of the saint's captivity as Slemish mountain in the modern County Antrim. While they undoubtedly embroidered their stories extravagantly and introduced many incredible legends and miracles there is no reason why they should have mistaken or falsified a place-name which would have impressed itself on Patrick's converts and had no other significance, either for the prestige of the church of Armagh or as a pagan place of worship like Croagh Patrick.

Slemish is about nine miles east of Ballymena and can be reached most conveniently from the Broughshane road from the small village of Buckna. The mountain rises to 1437 feet and commands a panoramic view of the heartland of Ulster. In Patrick's time the lower slopes were well wooded with fir or pine; their strong thick

roots remain today buried in the bog on the
eastern side of the mountain. Local farmers maintain that Patrick can have tended only sheep
on the mountain itself, that pigs and cattle
would have been confined to the lower slopes.
Another interesting detail they mention is that
he would never have done all the work himself.
Today it takes five men with dogs to bring down
the sheep from the mountain. Father Cummings,
C.Ss.R., who has written on Slemish in detail
(Furrow, March 1955) also suggests that Patrick
may have used the caves on the south-western
side which was sheltered from the icy blasts
of the north and east.

CHAPTER 3

THE CHANGING IMAGE

The oldest tribute to St Patrick which survives today is the well-known hymn *Audite Omnes* from the seventh century. The theme is lofty and rather tedious praise of the saint's virtues and we can be quite certain it would not have appealed to himself. The hymn is important historically because it marks the beginning of the vast literature which takes the saint from the realistic and credible pages of the *Confession* and the Coroticus letter and transforms him into a national hero of saga and folklore.

In the long history of devotion to Patrick the most remarkable period of all was the century after his death when he is virtually ignored in records. Prolific writers like Columbanus of Bangor and the Venerable Bede never mention Patrick at all even when they refer to the conversion of the Irish; Adomnan, the famous biographer of Colmcille, refers to him once briefly as "the holy bishop, Patrick". Throughout the seventh century there was a dramatic swing in

Patrick's favour. *Audite Omnes* was followed by
the biographies of Muirchú and Tíreachán and
the saint's reputation was secure for all time.
Many popular prayers like the *Breastplate* were
associated with his authorship; only in recent
years have scholars recognised this as an eighth-
century charm to be recited before a journey.
The *Tripartite Life* finally brought Patrick into
contact with every part of the country about
the end of the ninth century and leaves us in no
doubt of his unchallenged stature as the first
Apostle of Ireland.

The twelfth-century reform of Church life
and spirituality gave devotion to Patrick a new
impetus. The Anglo-Normans who invaded the
country towards the end of this century were
anxious to use the Irish saints in order to
consolidate themselves; among the monks
who came with them there was genuine
interest as well. From this period we can trace
the development of Lough Derg and Downpatrick as Patrician shrines. Jocelin's *Life* was
the last of the series set in motion by Muirchú
four centuries earlier; in the words of Bieler
"with Jocelin the Patrick legend had reached
its full development".[1]

As in the general history of Europe and the
Church the modern era dates from the sixteenth century. The Renaissance provoked an entirely
new critical spirit which questioned the whole
basis and role of saints in Christian worship.
Both the controversies of the Protestant
Reformation and the reforms of the Council

1. The life and legend of Saint Patrick (Dublin 1949), p. 124

of Trent indirectly inspired study of Patrick
which moved away gradually from the naiveté
of the miracles and concentrated on efforts to
analyse the historical evidence. In the seventeenth century important work was published by
Archbishop James Ussher of Armagh and his
pupil Sir James Ware on the Protestant side, and
by the Donegal Franciscan John Colgan and the
Bollandist Daniel Papebroch for the Catholics.

Patrick's place in the liturgy of the Tridentine
Church was canonised formally when his feast
was inserted in the Roman Breviary. Also in this
century — 1681 is the exact year — we have our
earliest reference to the wearing of shamrock on
St Patrick's Day. The following century brought
the trend to give the saint's feast the gala
atmosphere of Irish music and "greenery" which
survives today, especially among Irish emigrants.
The later Frank O'Connor found a whole conception
of national identity signified by a late eighteenth-
century song seldom heard nowadays, *The Wearin'
of the Green.* "This little song", he wrote, "written
in pseudo-Irish dialect, probably by an Ulster
Presbyterian, and set to what seems to be an
adaptation of a Scottish pibroch, is our real
national anthem."[2] Finally, the instance of Patrick
as the most common Christian name in Ireland
seems to date from the seventeenth century. If
the index to the Annals of Ulster is any indication,
the form of the name almost exclusively in use
before 1600 was Giolla Pádraig (the servant of
Patrick) but this was by no means as frequent as
Patrick became later.

2. A book of Ireland (London 1959), p.22

APPENDIX ONE

CONFESSIO

1. Ego Patricius peccator rusticissimus et minimus omnium fidelium et contemptibilissimus apud plurimos patrem habui Calpornium diaconum filium quendam Potiti presbyteri, qui fuit uico Bannauen Taberniae*; uillulam enim prope habuit, ubi ego capturam dedi. Annorum eram tunc fere sedecim. Deum enim uerum ignorabam et Hiberione in captiuitate adductus sum cum tot milia hominum — secundum merita nostra, quia *a Deo recessimus* et *praecepta eius non custod-iuimus* et sacerdotibus nostris non oboedientes fuimus, qui [nos] nostram salutem admonebant: et Dominus *induxit super nos iram animationis suae et dispersit nos in gentibus* multis etiam *usque ad ultimum terrae,* ubi nunc paruitas mea esse uidetur inter alienigenas,

2. et ibi *Dominus aperuit sensum incredulitatis meae,* ut uel sero rememorarem delicta mea et ut *conuerterem toto corde ad Dominum Deum meum,* qui *respexit humilitatem meam* et misertus est adolescentiae et ignorantiae meae et custod-

---

*Sic Book of Armagh. *bannauem taburniae* Bieler.

iuit me antequam scirem eum et antequam saperem
uel distinguerem inter bonum et malum et muniuit
me et consolatus est me ut pater filium.

3. Vnde autem tacere non possum, *neque expedit
quidem,* tanta beneficia et tantam gratiam quam
mihi Dominus praestare dignatus est *in terra
captiuitatis meae;* quia haec est retributio nostra,
ut post correptionem uel agnitionem Dei *exaltare
et confiteri mirabilia eius* coram *omni natione
quae est sub omni caeli.*

4. Quia non est alius Deus nec umquam fuit nec
ante nec erit post haec praeter Deum Patrem
ingenitum, sine principio, a quo est omne principium, omnia tenentem, ut didicimus; et huius
filium Iesum Christum, quem cum Patre scilicet
semper fuisse testamur, ante originem saeculi
spiritaliter apud Patrem [et] inenarrabiliter
genitum ante omne principium, et per ipsum
facta sunt uisibilia et inuisibilia, hominem factum,
morte deuicta in caelis ad Patrem receptum, *et
dedit illi omnem potestatem super omne nomen
caelestium et terrestrium et infernorum et omnis
lingua confiteatur ei quia Dominus et Deus est
Iesus Christus,* quem credimus et expectamus
aduentum ipsius mox futurum, *iudex uiuorum
atque mortuorum, qui reddet unicuique secundum
facta sua;* et *effudit in nobis habunde Spiritum
Sanctum, donum* et *pignus* inmortalitatis, qui
facit credentes et oboedientes ut sint *filii Dei* et
coheredes Christi: quem confitemur et adoramus
unum Deum in trinitate sacri nominis.

5. Ipse enim dixit per prophetam: *Inuoca me in die tribulationis tuae et liberabo te et magnificabis me.* Et iterum inquit: *Opera autem Dei reuelare et confiteri honorificum est.*

6. Tamen etsi in multis imperfectus sum opto *fratribus et cognatis* meis scire qualitatem meam, ut possint perspicere uotum animae meae.

7. Non ignoro *testimonium Domini mei,* qui in psalmo testatur: *Perdes eos qui loquuntur men-dacium.* Et iterum inquit: *Os quod mentitur occidit animam.* Et idem Dominus in euangelio inquit: *Verbum otiosum quod locuti fuerint homines reddent pro eo rationem in die iudicii.*

8. Vnde autem uehementer debueram *cum timore et tremore* metuere hanc sententiam in die illa ubi nemo se poterit subtrahere uel abscondere, sed omnes omnino *reddituri sumus rationem* etiam minimorum peccatorum *ante tribunal Domini Christi.*

9. Quapropter olim cogitaui scibere, sed et usque nunc haesitaui; timui enim ne *incederem in linguam* hominum, quia non didici sicut et ceteri, qui optime itaque iura et sacras litteras utraque pari modo combiberunt et sermones illorum ex infantia numquam mutarunt, sed magis ad perfectum semper addiderunt. Nam *sermo et loquela* nostra translata est in linguam alienam, sicut facile potest probari ex saliua scripturae meae qualiter sum ego in sermonibus instructus

atque eruditus, quia, inquit, *sapiens per linguam
dinoscetur et sensus et scientia et doctrina ueritatis.*

10. Sed quid prodest excusatio *iuxta ueritatem,*
praesertim cum praesumptione, quatenus modo
ipse adpeto in senectute mea quod in iuuentute
non comparaui? quod obstiterunt peccata mea ut
confirmarem quod ante perlegeram. Sed quis me
credit etsi dixero quod ante praefatus sum?

Adolescens, immo paene puer in uerbis*, capturam dedi, antequam scirem quid adpetere uel
quid uitare debueram. Vnde ergo hodie erubesco
et uehementer pertimeo denudare imperitiam
meam, quia desertis breuitate sermone explicare
nequeo, sicut enim spiritus gestit et animus, et
sensus monstrat adfectus.

11. Sed si itaque datum mihi fuisset sicut et
ceteris, uerumtamen non silerem *propter retribut-
ionem,* et si forte uidetur apud aliquantos me in
hoc praeponere cum mea inscientia et *tardiori
lingua,* sed etiam scriptum est enim: *Linguae
balbutientes uelociter discent loqui pacem.*

Quanto magis nos adpetere debemus, qui
sumus, inquit, *epistola Christi in salutem usque
ad ultimum terrae,* et si non deserta, sed ratum
et fortissimum *scripta in cordibus uestris non
atramento sed spiritu Dei uiui.* Et iterum Spiritus
testatur *et rusticationem ab Altissimo creatam.*

12. Vnde ego primus rusticus profuga indoctus
scilicet, *qui nescio in posterum prouidere,* sed
illud scio certissime quia utique *priusquam*

*inuerbis Bieler.

humiliarer ego eram uelut lapis qui iacet in *luto
profundo:* et uenit *qui potens est* et in sua
misericordia sustulit me et quidem scilicet
sursum adleuauit et collocauit me in summo
pariete; et inde fortiter debueram exclamare ad
retribuendum quoque aliquid Domino pro tantis
beneficiis eius hic et in aeternum, quae mens
hominum aestimare non potest.

13. Vnde autem ammiramini itaque *magni et
pusilli qui timetis Deum* et uos dominicati rethorici
audite et scrutamini. Quis me stultum excitauit
de medio eorum qui uidentur esse sapientes et
legis periti et *potentes in sermone* et in omni re,
et me quidem, detestabilis huius mundi, prae
ceteris inspirauit si talis essem — dummodo autem —
ut *cum metu et reuerentia* et *sine querella*
fideliter prodessem genti ad quam *caritas Christi*
transtulit et donauit me in uita mea, si dignus fuero,
denique et cum humilitate et ueraciter deseruirem
illis.

14. In mensura itaque fidei Trinitatis oportet
distinguere, sine reprehensione periculi notum
facere *donum Dei* et consolationem aeternam,
sine timore fiducialiter Dei nomen ubique expand-
ere, ut etiam *post obitum meum* exaga[e]llias
relinquere fratribus et filiis meis quos in Domino ego
baptizaui tot milia hominum—

(15) et non eram dignus neque talis ut hoc
Dominus seruulo suo concederet, post aerumnas
et tantas moles, post captiuitatem, post annos

multos in gentem illam tantam gratiam mihi
donaret; quod ego aliquando in iuuentute mea
numquam speraui neque cogitaui.

16. Sed postquam Hiberione deueneram — cotidie
itaque pecora pascebam et frequens in die orabam
— magis ac magis accedebat amor Dei et timor
ipsius et fides augebatur et spiritus agebatur, ut
in die una usque ad centum orationes et in
nocte prope similiter, ut etiam in siluis et monte
manebam, et ante lucem excitabar ad orationem
per niuem per gelu per pluuiam, et nihil mali sentie-
bam neque ulla pigritia erat in me — sicut modo
uideo, quia tunc spiritus in me feruebat —

(17) et ibi scilicet quadam nocte in somno audiui
uocem dicentem mihi: 'Bene ieiunas cito iturus
ad patriam tuam,' et iterum post paululum
tempus audiui *responsum* dicentem mihi: 'Ecce
nauis tua parata est' — et non erat prope, sed
forte habebat ducenta milia passus et ibi numquam fueram nec ibi notum quemquam de
hominibus habebam — et deinde postmodum
conuersus sum in fugam et intermisi hominem
cum quo fueram sex annis et ueni in uirtute Dei,
qui uiam meam ad bonum dirigebat et nihil
metuebam donec perueni ad nauem illam,

(18) et illa die qua perueni profecta est nauis de
loco suo, et locutus sum ut haberem unde
nauigare cum illis et gubernator displicuit illi et
acriter cum indignatione respondit: 'Nequaquam
tu nobiscum adpetes ire,' et cum haec audiissem

separaui me ab illis ut uenirem ad tegoriolum ubi
hospitabam, et in itinere coepi orare et antequam
orationem consummarem audiui unum ex illis et
fortiter exclamabat post me: 'Veni cito, quia
uocant te homines isti,' et statim ad illos reuersus
sum, et coeperunt mihi dicere: 'Veni, quia ex
fide recipimus te; fac nobiscum amicitiam quo
modo uolueris' — et in illa die itaque reppuli
sugere mammellas eorum propter timorem Dei,
sed uerumtamen ab illis speraui uenire in fidem
Iesu Christi, quia gentes erant — et ob hoc obtinui
cum illis, et protinus nauigauimus,

(19) et post triduum terram cepimus et uiginti
octo dies per desertum iter fecimus et cibus defuit
illis et *fames inualuit super eos,* et alio die coepit
gubernator mihi dicere: 'Quid est, Christiane? tu
dicis deus tuus magnus et omnipotens est; quare
ergo non potes pro nobis orare? quia nos a fame
periclitamur, difficile est enim ut aliquem hominem
umquam uideamus.' Ego enim confidenter dixi
illis: *'Conuertimini* ex fide *ex toto corde ad
Dominum Deum meum, quia nihil est impossibile
illi,* ut hodie cibum mittat uobis in uiam uestram
usque dum satiamini, quia ubique habundat illi,'
et adiuuante Deo ita factum est: ecce grex
porcorum in uia ante oculos nostros apparuit, et
multos ex illis interfecerunt et ibi duas noctes
manserunt et bene refecti et canes eorum repleti
sunt, quia multi ex illis *defecerunt* et secus uiam
semiuiui relicti sunt, et post hoc summas gratias
egerunt Deo et ego honorificatus sum sub oculis
eorum, et ex hac die cibum habundanter habuerunt;

etiam *mel siluestre* inuenerunt et *mihi partem
obtulerunt* et unus ex illis dixit: *'Immolaticium
est';* Deo gratias, exinde nihil gustaui.

22. Etiam in itinere praeuidit nobis cibum et
ignem et siccitatem cotidie donec decimo die
peruenimus homines. Sicut superius insinuaui,
uiginti et octo dies per desertum iter fecimus et
ea nocte qua peruenimus homines de cibo
uero nihil habuimus.

20. Eadem uero nocte eram dormiens et fortiter
temptauit me satanas, quod memor ero *quamdiu
fuero in hoc corpore,* et cecidit super me ueluti
saxum ingens et nihil membrorum meorum
praeualens. Sed unde me uenit ignaro in spiritu
ut Heliam uocarem? Et inter haec uidi in caelum
solem oriri et dum clamarem 'Helia, Helia' uiribus
meis, ecce splendor solis illius decidit super me
et statim discussit a me omnem grauitudinem, et
credo quod a Christo Domino meo subuentus
sum et spiritus eius iam tunc clamabat pro me et
spero quod sic erit *in die pressurae* meae, sicut in
euangelio inquit: *In illa die,* Dominus testatur,
*non uos estis qui loquimini, sed spiritus Patris
uestri qui loquitur in uobis.*

21. Et iterum post annos multos adhuc capturam
dedi. Ea nocte prima itaque mansi cum illis.
Responsum autem *diuinum* audiui dicentem mihi:
'Duobus mensibus eris cum illis.' Quod ita factum
est: nocte illa sexagesima *liberauit me Dominus
de manibus eorum.*

23. Et iterum post paucos annos in Brittanniis eram cum parentibus meis, qui me ut filium susceperunt et ex fide rogauerunt me ut uel modo ego post tantas tribulationes quas ego pertuli nusquam ab illis discederem, et ibi scilicet *uidi in uisu noctis* uirum uenientem quasi de Hiberione, cui nomen Victoricus, cum epistolis innumerabilibus, et dedit mihi unam ex his et legi principium epistolae continentem 'Vox Hiberionacum,' et cum recitabam principium epistolae putabam ipso momento audire uocem ipsorum, qui erant iuxta siluam Vocluti quae est prope mare occidentale, et sic exclamauerunt *quasi ex uno ore:* 'Rogamus te, (sancte) puer, ut uenias et adhuc ambulas inter nos,' et ualde *compunctus sum corde* et amplius non potui legere et sic expertus sum. Deo gratias, quia post plurimos annos praestitit illis Dominus secundum clamorem illorum.

24. Et alia nocte — *nescio, Deus scit,* utrum in me an iuxta me — uerbis peritissime, quos ego audiui et non potui intellegere, nisi ad postremum orationis sic effitiatus est: *'Qui dedit animam suam pro te,* ipse est qui loquitur in te,' et sic expertus sum gaudibundus.

25. Et iterum uidi in me ipsum orantem et eram quasi intra corpus meum et audiui super me, hoc est super *interiorem hominem,* et ibi fortiter orabat gemitibus, et inter haec *stupebam et ammirabam et cogitabam* quis esset qui in me orabat, sed ad postremum orationis sic effitiatus est ut sit Spiritus, et sic expertus sum et record-

atus sum apostolo dicente: *Spiritus adiuuat
infirmitates orationis nostrae: nam quod oremus
sicut oportet nescimus: sed ipse Spiritus postulat
pro nobis gemitibus inenarrabilibus, quae uerbis
exprimi non possunt;* et iterum: *Dominus aduocatus
noster postulat pro nobis.*

26. Et quando temptatus sum ab aliquantis senioribus meis, qui uenerunt, et peccata mea, contra
laboriosum episcopatum meum, utique illo die
fortiter *impulsus sum ut caderem* hic et in aeternum; sed Dominus pepercit proselito et peregrino
propter nomen suum benigne et ualde mihi subuenit
in hac conculcatione. Quod in labe et in obprobrium
non male deueni! Deum oro ut *non illis in pecca-
tum reputetur occasio.*

27. Nam* post annos triginta *inuenerunt me
aduersus* uerbum quod confessus fueram antequam essem diaconus. Propter anxietatem maesto
animo insinuaui amicissimo meo quae in pueritia
mea una die gesseram, immo in una hora, quia
necdum praeualebam. *Nescio, Deus scit,* si habebam tunc annos quindecim, et Deum uiuum non
credebam, neque ex infantia mea, sed in morte et
in incredulitate mansi donec ualde castigatus sum
et in ueritate humiliatus sum a fame et nuditate,
et cotidie,

(28) contra, Hiberione non sponte pergebam, *donec*
prope *deficiebam**. Sed hoc potius bene mihi fuit,
qui ex hoc emendatus sum a Domino, et aptauit
me ut hodie essem quod aliquando longe a me

---

*Sic Bollandists. *Occasionem* Bieler. *Occasionum* Mss.
*Punctuation of this sentence differs from Bieler.

erat, ut ego curam haberem aut satagerem pro
salute aliorum, quando autem tunc etiam de me
ipso non cogitabam.

29. Igitur in illo die quo *reprobatus sum* a memoratis
supradictis ad noctem illam *uidi in uisu noctis*
scriptum erat contra faciem meam sine honore,
et inter haec audiui *responsum diuinum* dicentem
mihi: Male uidimus faciem designati nudato nomine,
nec sic praedixit: Male uidisti, sed: Male uidimus,
quasi sibi se iunxisset, sicut dixit: *Qui uos tangit
quasi qui tangit pupillam oculi mei.*

30. Idcirco *gratias ago ei qui me* in omnibus *con-
fortauit,* ut non me impediret a profectione quam
statueram et de mea quoque opera quod a Christo
Domino meo didiceram, sed magis ex eo *sensi in
me uirtutem* non paruam et fides mea probata est
coram Deo et hominibus.

31. Vnde autem *audenter dico* non me reprehendit
conscientia mea hic et in futurum: *teste Deo* habeo
quia non sum mentitus in sermonibus quos ego
retuli uobis.

32. Sed magis doleo pro amicissimo meo cur hoc
meruimus audire tale responsum. Cui ego credidi
etiam animam! Et comperi ab aliquantis fratribus
ante defensionem illam (quod ego non interfui
nec in Brittanniis eram nec a me orietur*) ut et ille
in mea absentia pulsaret pro me; etiam mihi ipse
ore suo dixerat: 'Ecce dandus es tu ad gradum

*Sic Mss. Cf. O Raifeartaigh *Ir. Eccl. Rec.* (Oct.1967) 209.

episcopatus,' quod non eram dignus. Sed unde
uenit illi postmodum ut coram cunctis, bonis et
malis, et me publice dehonestaret quod ante
sponte et laetus indulserat, et Dominus, qui
maior omnibus est?

33. Satis dico. Sed tamen non debeo abscondere
donum Dei quod largitus est nobis *in terra
captiuitatis meae,* quia tunc fortiter inquisiui eum
et ibi inueni illum et seruauit me ab omnibus
iniquitatibus (sic credo) *propter inhabitantem
Spiritum* eius, qui *operatus est* usque in hanc diem
in me. *Audenter* rursus. Sed scit Deus, si mihi
homo hoc effatus fuisset, forsitan tacuissem
propter *caritatem Christi.*

34. Vnde ergo indefessam gratiam ago Deo meo,
qui me fidelem seruauit *in die temptationis meae,*
ita ut hodie confidenter offeram illi sacrificium ut
hostiam uiuentem animam meam Christo Domino
meo, qui me *seruauit ab omnibus angustiis meis,*
ut et dicam: *Quis ego sum, Domine,* uel quae est
uocatio mea, qui mihi tanta diuinitate cooperasti,
ita ut hodie *in gentibus* constanter *exaltarem et
magnificarem nomen tuum* ubicumque loco fuero,
nec non in secundis sed etiam in pressuris, ut
quicquid mihi euenerit siue bonum siue malum
aequaliter debeo suscipere et Deo gratias semper
agere, qui mihi ostendit ut indubitabilem eum
sine fine crederem et qui me audierit ut ego inscius
et *in nouissimis diebus* hoc opus tam pium et tam
mirificum auderem adgredere, ita ut imitarem
quippiam illos quos ante Dominus iam olim

praedixerat praenuntiaturos euangelium suum
in testimonium omnibus gentibus ante *finem
mundi,* quod ita ergo uidimus itaque suppletum
est: ecce testes sumus quia euangelium prae-
dicatum est usque ubi nemo ultra est.

35. Longum est autem totum per singula enarrare
laborem meum uel per partes. Breuiter dicam qualiter
piissimus Deus de seruitute saepe liberauit et de
periculis duodecim qua periclitata est anima mea,
praeter insidias multas et *quae uerbis exprimere
non ualeo.* Nec iniuriam legentibus faciam;
sed Deum auctorem habeo, qui nouit omnia
etiam antequam fiant, ut me pauperculum
pupillum ideo tamen *responsum diuinum* creber
admonere.

36. *Vnde mihi haec sapientia,* quae in me non
erat, qui nec *numerum dierum noueram* neque
Deum sapiebam? Vnde mihi postmodum donum
tam magnum tam salubre Deum agnoscere uel
diligere, sed ut patriam et parentes amitterem?

37. Et munera multa mihi offerebantur cum fletu
et lacrimis et offendi illos, nec non contra uotum
aliquantis de senioribus meis, sed gubernante Deo nullo
modo consensi neque adquieui illis — non mea gratia,
sed Deus qui uincit in me et resistit illis omnibus, ut ego
ueneram ad Hibernas gentes euangelium praedicare
et ab incredulis contumelias perferre, ut *audirem
obprobrium peregrinationis meae,* et persecutiones
multas *usque ad uincula* et ut darem ingenuitat-

em meam pro utilitate aliorum et, si dignus fuero,
promptus sum ut etiam *animam meam* incunctanter
et *libentissime* pro nomine eius et ibi opto
impendere eam *usque ad mortem,* si Dominus
mihi indulgeret,

(38) quia ualde *debitor sum* Deo, qui mihi tantam
gratiam donauit ut populi multi per me in Deum
renascerentur et postmodum consummarentur
et ut clerici ubique illis ordinarentur ad plebem
nuper uenientem ad credulitatem, quam sumpsit
Dominus *ab extremis terrae,* sicut olim promiserat
per prophetas suos: *Ad te gentes uenient ab*
extremis terrae et dicent: sicut falsa comparauer-
unt patres nostri idola et non est in eis utilitas;
et iterum: *Posui te lumen in gentibus ut sis in*
salutem usque ad extremum terrae.

39. Et ibi uolo *expectare promissum* ipsius, qui
utique numquam fallit, sicut in euangelio pollicetur:
Venient ab oriente et occidente et recumbent
cum Abraam et Isaac et Iacob, sicut credimus
ab omni mundo uenturi sunt credentes.

40. Idcirco itaque oportet quidem bene et diligenter piscare, sicut Dominus praemonet et docet
dicens: *Venite post me et faciam fieri uos*
piscatores hominum; et iterum dicit per prophetas:
Ecce mitto piscatores et uenatores multos, dicit
Deus, et cetera.
Vnde autem ualde oportebat retia nostra tendere,
ita ut *multitudo copiosa et turba* Deo caperetur
et ubique essent clerici qui baptizarent et exhort-

arent populum indigentem et desiderantem, sicut
Dominus inquit in euangelio, ammonet et docet
dicens: *Euntes ergo nunc docete omnes gentes*
baptizantes eas in nomine Patris et Filii et
Spiritus Sancti docentes eos obseruare omnia
quaecumque mandaui uobis: et ecce ego uobiscum
sum omnibus diebus usque ad consummationem
saeculi; et iterum dicit: *Euntes ergo in mundum*
uniuersum praedicate euangelium omni creaturae;
qui crediderit et baptizatus fuerit saluus erit; qui
uero non crediderit condempnabitur; et iterum:
Praedicabitur hoc euangelium regni in uniuerso
mundo in testimonium omnibus gentibus et tunc
ueniet finis; et item Dominus per prophetam
praenuntiat inquit: *Et erit in nouissimis diebus,*
dicit Dominus, effundam de spiritu meo super
omnem carnem et prophetabunt filii uestri et
filiae uestrae et iuuenes uestri uisiones uidebunt
et seniores uestri somnia somniabunt et quidem
super seruos meos et super ancillas meas in diebus
illis effundam de spiritu meo et prophetabunt;
et *in Osee dicit: Vocabo non plebem meam plebem*
meam et non misericordiam consecutam misericor-
diam consecutam et erit in loco ubi dictum est:
Non plebs mea uos, ibi uocabuntur filii Dei uiui.

41. Vnde autem Hiberione qui numquam notitiam
Dei habuerunt nisi idola et inmunda usque nunc
semper coluerunt quomodo *nuper facta est plebs*
Domini et filii Dei nuncupantur, filii Scottorum
et filiae regulorum monachi et uirgines Christi
esse uidentur?

42. Et etiam una benedicta Scotta genetiua
nobilis pulcherrima adulta erat, quam ego
baptizaui; et post paucos dies una causa uenit ad
nos, insinuauit nobis responsum accepisse a nuntio
Dei et monuit eam ut esset uirgo Christi et ipsa
Deo proximaret: Deo gratias, sexta ab hac die
optime et auidissime arripuit illud quod etiam
omnes uirgines Dei ita hoc faciunt — non sponte
patrum earum, sed et persecutiones patiuntur et
improperia falsa a parentibus suis et nihilominus
plus augetur numerus (et de genere nostro qui ibi
nati sunt nescimus numerum eorum) praeter
uiduas et continentes. Sed ex illis maxime laborant
quae seruitio detinentur: usque ad terrores et
minas assidue perferunt; sed Dominus gratiam
dedit multis ex ancillis suis, nam etsi uetantur
tamen fortiter imitantur.

43. Vnde autem etsi uoluero amittere illas et ut
pergens in Brittanniis — et libentissime *paratus
eram* quasi ad patriam et parentes; non id solum sed
etiam usque ad Gallias uisitare fratres et ut uiderem
faciem sanctorum Domini mei: scit Deus quod ego
ualde optabam, sed *alligatus Spiritu,* qui mihi
protestatur si hoc fecero, ut futurum reum me esse
designat et timeo perdere laborem quem inchoaui, et
non ego sed Christus Dominus, qui me imperauit ut
uenirem esse cum illis residuum aetatis meae, *si
Dominus uoluerit* et custodierit me ab omni uia mala,
ut non *peccem coram illo;*

(44) spero autem hoc debueram, sed memet ipsum
non credo *quamdiu fuero in hoc corpore mortis,*

quia fortis est qui cotidie nititur subuertere me
a fide et praeposita castitate religionis non fictae
usque in finem uitae meae Christo Domino meo,
sed *caro inimica* semper trahit ad mortem, id est
ad inlecebras inlicitate perficiendas; et *scio ex
parte* quare uitam perfectam ego non egi sicut et
ceteri credentes, sed confiteor Domino meo, et
non erubesco in conspectu ipsius, *quia non mentior,*
ex quo cognoui eum *a iuuentute mea* creuit in
me amor Dei et timor ipsius, *et usque nunc*
fauente Domino *fidem seruaui.*

45. Rideat autem et insultet qui uoluerit, ego non
silebo neque abscondo signa et mirabilia quae
mihi a Domino monstrata sunt ante multos annos
quam fierent, quasi qui nouit omnia etiam *ante
tempora saecularia.*

46. Vnde autem debueram sine cessatione Deo
gratias agere, qui saepe indulsit insipientiae meae
neglegentiae meae et de loco non in uno quoque
ut non mihi uehementer irasceretur, qui adiutor
datus sum et non cito adquieui secundum quod
mihi ostensum fuerat et sicut *Spiritus suggerebat,*
et *misertus est* mihi Dominus *in milia milium,*
quia uidit in me quod *paratus eram,* sed quod
mihi pro his nesciebam de statu meo quid facerem,
quia multi hanc legationem prohibebant, etiam
inter se ipsos pos tergum meum narrabant et
dicebant: 'Iste quare se mittit in periculo inter
hostes qui Deum non nouerunt? — non ut causa
malitiae, sed non sapiebat illis, sicut et ego ipse
testor, intellegi propter rusticitatem meam — et

non cito agnoui gratiam quae tunc erat in me;
nunc mihi sapit quod ante debueram.

47. Nunc ergo simpliciter insinuaui fratribus et
conseruis meis qui mihi crediderunt propter quod
praedixi et praedico ad roborandam et confirm-
andam fidem uestram. Vtinam ut et uos imitemini
maiora et potiora faciatis! Hoc erit gloria mea,
quia *filius sapiens gloria patris est.*

48. Vos scitis et Deus qualiter inter uos conuersatus
sum *a iuuentute mea* in fide ueritatis *et in sincer-
itate cordis.* Etiam ad gentes illas inter quas habito,
ego fidem illis praestaui et praestabo. Deus scit
neminem illorum *circumueni,* nec cogito, propter
Deum et ecclesiam ipsius, ne *excitem* illis et nobis
omnibus *persecutionem* et ne per me blasphe-
maretur nomen Domini; quia scriptum est: *Vae
homini per quem nomen Domini blasphematur.*

49. Nam *etsi imperitus sum in omnibus* tamen
conatus sum quippiam seruare me etiam et
fratribus Christianis et uirginibus Christi et mulieri-
bus religiosis, quae mihi ultronea munuscula donabant
et super altare iactabant ex ornamentis suis et iterum
reddebam illis et aduersus me scandalizabantur
cur hoc faciebam; sed ego propter spem perenn-
itatis, ut me in omnibus caute propterea
conseruarem, ita ut [non] me in aliquo titulo
infideli caperent uel ministerium seruitutis meae
nec etiam in minimo incredulis locum darem
infamare siue detractare.

50. Forte autem quando baptizaui tot milia hominum sperauerim ab aliquo illorum uel dimidio scriptulae? *Dicite mihi et reddam uobis.* Aut quando ordinauit ubique Dominus clericos per modicitatem meam et ministerium gratis distribui illis, si poposci ab aliquo illorum uel pretium uel *calciamenti* mei, *dicite aduersus me et reddam uobis.*

Magis (51) ego *impendi pro* uobis ut me *caperent,* et inter uos et ubique pergebam causa uestra in multis periculis etiam usque ad exteras partes, ubi nemo ultra erat et ubi numquam aliquis peruenerat qui baptizaret aut clericos ordinaret aut populum consummaret: donante Domino diligenter et libentissime pro salute uestra omnia [. . .] generaui.

52. Interim praemia dabam regibus praeter quod dabam mercedem filiis ipsorum qui mecum ambulant, et nihilominus comprehenderunt me cum comitibus meis et illa die auidissime cupiebant interficere me, sed tempus nondum uenerat, et omnia quaecumque nobiscum inuenerunt rapuerunt illud et me ipsum ferro uinxerunt, et quarto-decimo die absoluit me Dominus de potestate eorum et quicquid nostrum fuit redditum est nobis propter Deum et *necessarios amicos* quos ante praeuidimus.

53. Vos autem experti estis quantum ego erogaui illis qui iudicabant *per omnes regiones* quos ego frequentius uisitabam. Censeo enim non minimum

quam pretium quindecim hominum distribui illis,
ita ut me *fruamini* et ego *uobis* semper *fruar* in
Deum. Non me paenitet nec satis est mihi: adhuc
impendo et superimpendam; potens est Dominus
ut det mihi postmodum ut meipsum *impendar
pro animabus uestris.*

54. Ecce *testem Deum inuoco in animam meam
quia non mentior:* nequė ut sit *occasio adulationis*
uel *auaritiae* scripserim uobis neque ut honorem
spero ab aliquo uestro; sufficit enim honor qui
nondum uidetur sed corde creditur; *fidelis* autem
qui promisit: numquam mentitur.

55. Sed uideo iam *in praesenti saeculo* me supra
modum exaltatum a Domino, et non eram dignus
neque talis ut hoc mihi praestaret, dum scio
certissime quod mihi melius conuenit paupertas
et calamitas quam diuitiae et diliciae (sed et
Christus Dominus pauper fuit *pro nobis,* ego
uero miser et infelix etsi opes uoluero iam non
habeo, *neque me ipsum iudico),* quia cotidie
spero aut internicionem aut circumueniri aut
redigi in seruitutem siue occasio cuiuslibet; *sed
nihil horum uereor* propter promissa caelorum,
quia iactaui meipsum in manus Dei omnipotentis,
qui ubique dominatur, sicut propheta dicit: *Iacta
cogitatum tuum in Deum et ipse te enutriet.*

56. Ecce nunc *commendo animam meam fidel-
issimo Deo* meo, *pro quo legationem fungor* in
ignobilitate mea, sed quia *personam non accipit*

et elegit me ad hoc officium ut *unus* essem *de suis
minimis* minister.

57. Vnde autem *retribuam illi pro   omnibus quae
retribuit mihi.* Sed quid dicam uel quid promittam
Domino meo, quia nihil ualeo nisi ipse mihi
dederit? Sed *scrutator corda et renes* quia satis
et nimis cupio et *paratus eram* ut donaret mihi
bibere calicem eius, sicut indulsit et ceteris
amantibus se.

58. Quapropter non contingat mihi a Deo meo ut
numquam amittam *plebem* suam *quam adquisiuit*
in ultimis terrae. Oro Deum ut det mihi perseuer-
antiam et dignetur ut reddam illi testem fidelem
usque ad transitum meum propter Deum meum,

(59) et si aliquid boni umquam imitatus sum
propter Deum meum, quem diligo, peto illi det
mihi ut cum illis proselitis et captiuis pro nomine
suo effundam sanguinem meum, etsi ipsam etiam
caream sepulturam aut miserissime cadauer per
singula membra diuidatur canibus aut bestiis
asperis aut *uolucres caeli comederent illud.*
Certissime reor, si mihi hoc incurrisset, lucratus
sum animam cum corpore meo, quia *sine ulla
dubitatione* in die illa *resurgemus* in claritate solis,
hoc est *in gloria* Christi Iesu redemptoris nostri,
quasi *filii Dei* uiui et *coheredes Christi et
conformes futuri imaginis ipsius;* quoniam *ex ipso
per ipsum et in ipso* regnaturi sumus.

60. Nam sol iste quem uidemus [ipso] iubente
propter nos cotidie oritur, sed numquam regnabit

neque permanebit splendor eius, sed et omnes
qui adorant eum in poenam miseri male deuenient;
nos autem, qui credimus et adoramus solem
uerum Christum, qui numquam interibit, neque
qui fecerit uoluntatem ipsius, sed *manebit in
aeternum quomodo et Christus manet in aeternum,*
qui regnat cum Deo Patre omnipotente et cum
Spiritu Sancto ante saecula et nunc et per omnia
saecula saeculorum, Amen.

61. Ecce iterum iterumque breuiter exponam
uerba confessionis meae. *Testificor* in ueritate et
in *exultatione cordis coram Deo et sanctis angelis
eius* quia numquam habui aliquam occasionem
praeter euangelium et promissa illius ut umquam
redirem ad gentem illam unde prius uix euaseram.

62. Sed precor credentibus et timentibus Deum,
quicumque dignatus fuerit inspicere uel recipere
hanc scripturam quam Patricius, peccator,
indoctus scilicet Hiberione conscripsit, ut nemo
umquam dicat quod mea ignorantia, si aliquid
pusillum egi uel demonstrauerim secundum Dei
placitum, sed arbitramini et uerissime credatur
quod *donum Dei* fuisset. Et haec est confessio
mea antequam moriar.

APPENDIX TWO

LETTER TO THE SOLDIERS
OF COROTICUS

PATRICK'S RIGHT TO PROTEST

I, Patrick, an unlearned sinner, resident in Ireland, declare myself to be a bishop. I believe most firmly that what I am I have received from God. That is why I live among uncivilised people, a stranger and exile for the love of God. He is my witness that this is so. Not that I have usually wanted to speak out in such a severe harsh way. But I am compelled by concern for God. The truth of Christ has aroused me, out of love for my neighbours and children, for whom I have given up country and kinsfolk, and my own life even to death. If I am worthy, I live only for God to teach the nations, even though some despise me.

With my own hand I have written down these words. I composed them to be related and passed on, in order that they may be sent to the soldiers of Coroticus. I do not say to my fellow-citizens or to the fellow-citizens of the holy Romans but to the fellow-citizens of the devils, because of their evil actions. In their hostile behaviour they live in death, these allies of the Scots and apostate Picts. Dripping with blood they wallow in the slaughter of innocent Christians, whom I personally brought into the life of the baptised and confirmed in Christ.

The newly-baptized in their white garments had just been anointed with chrism. It was still giving forth its scent on their foreheads when they were cruelly and brutally murdered, put to the sword by these men I have already mentioned. The next day I sent a letter with a holy presbyter in the company of clergy, a man I had taught from his childhood. We wanted something saved from the plunder, some of the baptized prisoners spared. They made fun of them.

THE SIN MUST BE PUNISHED

Consequently, I do not know for whom I am to grieve more bitterly; whether for those who were killed, for those whom they captured, or those whom the Devil had deeply ensnared. For everyone who commits sin is a slave and is called a child of the Devil. Therefore, let every God-fearing man know that they are strangers from me and from Christ my God, whose ambassador I am. They are murderers of father and of brother, fierce wolves devouring the people of the Lord as they would devour bread. As Scripture says: Lord, the wicked have broken your law, your law which but recently he had in his kindness successfully planted in Ireland, and which had established itself by his divine grace.

I made no false claim. My lot is with those whom he called and predestined to preach the Gospel among bitter persecutions even to the ends of the earth. I do this even though the Enemy shows his

jealousy through the tyranny of Coroticus, a man
without respect either for God or for his bishops
whom he chose and graciously granted the highest
form of supreme divine power, that those whom
they bind on earth should be bound also in heaven.

So, I make these special requests of you, devout
and humble-hearted men. It is not permitted to
court the favour of such people, to take food or
drink with them, or even to accept their alms. They
must first make reparation to God through rigorous
penance and in floods of tears. They must have
freed the servants of God and baptized handmaids
of Christ, for whom he died and was crucified.

Scripture says: The Most High takes no pleasure
in offerings from the wicked. Offering sacrifice from
the property of the poor is just as evil as
slaughtering a son in the presence of his father.
Riches which the wicked man has unjustly gathered
will be disgorged from his bellly, the angel of death
will drag him away, he will be tormented by the
rage of dragons, the tongue of the viper will kill him
and unquenchable fire consume him. Woe to those
who amass goods which are not their own. What
will a man gain if he wins the whole world and
suffers the loss of his own life?

It would be tedious to discuss or to mention every
text, to gather proofs from the whole Law relating
to such greed. Avarice is a deadly sin. You shall not
covet your neighbour's property. You shall not kill.
A murderer cannot be with Christ. He who hates
his brother is to be considered a murderer. He who
does not love his brother remains in death. How
much more guilty is he who has stained his hands

with the blood of the children of God whom he has
recently gathered at the ends of the earth through
my poor preaching?

PATRICK ISOLATED

Surely it was not without God or for worldly
purposes that I came to Ireland? Who compelled
me? I am bound by the Spirit not to see any of my
relatives. Surely it is not from myself that my
ministry of mercy to that people derives, that people
who once kidnapped me and made away with the
men and women servants of my father's house? I
was born free in worldly status. My father was a
decurion. But I sold my birthright without shame or
regret for the benefit of others. Thus I am a servant
in Christ to a far-off nation on account of the
indescribable glory of eternal life which is in Christ
Jesus our Lord.

And if my own people do not recognise me, there
is no respect for a prophet in his own country.
Perhaps we do not belong to the same fold and do
not have the same God as Father. And: He who
does not gather with me scatters. It is not right that
one man pulls down while another builds up. I do
not seek what is my own. It is not my virtue but
God who puts this concern into my heart that I
should become one of the huntsmen or fishermen
whom God once foretold would come in the last
days.

I am in a hateful position. What am I to do,
Lord? I am greatly despised. Look, your sheep are

mangled and carried off in my presence, and by
those robbers at the bidding of the enemy
Coroticus. Far from the love of God is the betrayer
of Christians into the hands of the Scots and the
Picts. Fierce wolves have swallowed up the Lord's
flock which was increasing well in Ireland as a
result of steady work, countless sons of Scots and
princesses have become monks and virgins for
Christ. For this reason may the wrong done to the
just find no pleasure with you, Lord. Indeed at no
stage will it please you as it makes its ways to hell.

MURDER FOR MONEY

Which of the faithful would not shrink from
making merry or enjoying good cheer with people of
this sort? They have filled their houses with the
spoils of dead Christians, they make their living on
plunder. The wretches do not know that what they
are offering as food to their friends and children is
deadly poison, just as Eve did not understand that it
was death she was offering her husband. So are all
who do evil: they bring about eternal death as their
punishment.

This is the custom of the Roman Christians in
Gaul: they send suitably holy men to the Franks
and the other nations with so many thousands of
shillings to ransom baptized prisoners. But you, on
the contrary, murder them and sell them to a far-off
nation that does not know God. You hand over the
members of Christ into what could be called a
brothel. What hope have you in God, or anyone

who thinks like you or converses with you in words of flattery? God will judge. For it is written: Not only those who do evil things but those who consent to them are to be condemned.

GRIEF AND CONSOLATION

I do not know what I am to say or speak further about those departed children, whom the sword struck down all too harshly. For it is written: Be sad with those in sorrow. And elsewhere: If any member grieves, let all the members grieve as well. Therefore, the Church mourns and laments her sons and daughters whom the sword has not yet killed, but who are in exile, having been carried away into distant lands where serious and shameless sin openly abounds. Free men are sold there as slaves, Christians reduced to slavery, and worst of all, given over to the most worthless, vilest and apostate Picts.

Therefore, I will cry aloud in sorrow and grief: Most dearly beloved brothers and children, the fairest of the host I begot in Christ, what can I do for you? I am not worthy to come to the help of either God or man. The wickedness of the wicked has prevailed over us. We have become like strangers. Perhaps they do not believe that we have received one and the same baptism, that we have one and the same God as Father. They think it a disgrace that we are Irish. Scripture says: Have you not all one God? Why has each one of you deserted his neighbour?

Therefore, I lament for you, I lament, my dearly beloved. But again, I rejoice in my heart. I have not laboured for nothing: my travels have not been in vain. And if this outrage, so dreadful, so unspeakable, has to happen, then God be thanked that you have left this world for Paradise as baptized Christians. I can see you: You have begun to journey where night will be no more, nor mourning, nor death. But you will leap like calves freed from the tether: you will trample on the wicked and they will be like ashes under your feet.

You will reign with apostles and prophets and martyrs. You will receive everlasting kingdoms. As he himself testifies, saying: They will come from east and west and will take their places with Abraham and Isaac and Jacob in the kingdom of heaven.

THE SINNER MUST REPENT

Outside are dogs and sorcerers and murderers. As for liars and perjurers, their lot is in the lake of everlasting fire. It is not without justice that the Apostle says: If it is hard for a good man to be saved, where will the sinner and reckless lawbreaker find himself?

And as for Coroticus and his criminals, rebels against Christ, where will they find themselves, men who distribute baptized women as spoil in the service of a vile earthly kingdom which may of course disappear in a moment? Like a cloud of smoke dispersed by the wind, deceitful sinners will perish when God approaches. But good men will feast with Christ without interruption, they will judge nations and they will rule over wicked kings for ever and ever. Amen.

I protest before God and his angels that it will happen as he has indicated to me, ignored though I may be. These are not my words which I have set out in Latin, but the words of God and of apostles and prophets: and they have never told lies. He who will believe will be saved, but he who will not believe will be condemned. God has spoken.

I earnestly request the servant of God who shall volunteer to be the bearer of this letter, that on no account should it be suppressed or hidden by anyone, but rather that it should be read before all the people and in the presence of Coroticus himself. May God inspire them that at some time or other they may come to their senses again in his regard, that they may repent, even at the last minute, of their wicked crime — murder against the brothers of the Lord — and that they may free the baptized women prisoners whom they have already captured, so that they may deserve to live to God and be made well, now and in eternity.

Peace to the Father, and to the Son, and to the Holy Spirit. Amen.

1 Patrick wrote another letter, to the soldiers of
the Welsh chief, Coroticus, where he tells us that
Calpornius was a *decurio* or city councillor and
that he had a household of servants who were
killed in the raid.

   Sacerdos at this period can mean either a bishop
or priest.

9-10 Patrick's mother tongue was Vulgar Latin
which would have been mastered by him as a
literary medium had he avoided captivity or even
got down seriously to his studies after his escape.
While his schoolmates were being coached in
Latin grammar and syntax Patrick was grappling
with the foreign language of the Celtic-speaking
Irish.

18   Patrick describes his encounter with the
sailors only because of the religious significance
of the oath of loyalty he had to take. He refused
the pagan ritual of sucking the nipples and was
eventually allowed to substitute his own Christian
oath. The sacrifice of the wild honey is a similar
reference to pagan ceremony repugnant to
Patrick (19).

22   Although there is no MS. authority for this
transposition before the Bollandist edition of the
17th century it seems to be demanded by the
context and simply means that two sentences

were inadvertently omitted by an early copyist
and then inserted at the end of the section. The
reference to food links 19-22 and that to night
22-20.

20   The linking of the sun with Elijah and Christ
indicates Patrick's efforts to convert the Irish
from sun-worship which he mentions explicitly
in 60. He seems to be playing on the similarity
of the Greek word for the sun *(Helios)* and the
prophet's name in Latin *(Helias)*.

The "few years later" refer to 17-20 rather
than to 21 which is merely a tailpiece to the main
narrative. As is clear from the introduction,
Patrick is more concerned to associate ideas than
to observe time sequence in his writing.

23   The other examples of *puer* or *pueritia* in
Patrick's writings also emphasise his tender years
when he first came to Ireland (10) or before he
came at all (27). Referring elsewhere to his
captivity he describes himself as *adolescens*
(youth) or *iuventus* (young man).

25   Father Noel-Dermot O'Donoghue O.D.C.
comments: "This is one of the most remarkable
passages in Christian hagiography. The Apostle
of Ireland has been given exactly the same
experience as that which the Apostle of the
Gentiles recounts in this famous and rather
mysterious passage of the Epistle to the Romans."
(Studies Vol. L, 1961, p.161).

Patrick returns to the subject of his captivity
as the price he paid for conversion.

43 "Christian Community" translates "sanctorum
Domini mei". St Paul refers to members of the
Christian communities as saints exx. 2 Cor. 9:12,
13:12; Eph. 6:18; as indeed does Patrick again in
his Coroticus letter (13).

47-48 The "fellow-captives" *(conservi)* were
Patrick's missionary companions who also undertook voluntary exile and loss of free-born status
as Roman citizens (37). Patrick first addresses
his converts, his children as he had already called
them (14), and then directs his remarks in 48
to the *fratres et conservi* who have known him
since early manhood.

50 In his Coroticus letter (3) Patrick mentions
that the baptism ceremony included anointing
with chrism on the forehead and the wearing of
white garments.

A *scriptula* or *scrupulum* was a small silver
coin, one twenty-fourth part of an ounce.

53 The price of a man was the ransom demanded
for a prisoner. There is an interesting reference to
this practice in the Coroticus letter (14): "This is
the custom of Roman Christians among the Gauls:
they send suitable holy men to the Franks and
the other nations with so many thousands of *solidi*
to ransom baptised prisoners."